AF706251

# JUDICIAL INJUSTICE

## Unveiling the Power Divide

FD WURIEE

Angeles Publishers©

London England

**ISBN: 9798224173983**

© FD Wuriee © Angeles Publishers 2024

The Moral Rights of the Author have been asserted.

ALL RIGHTS RESERVED. No Part of this book may be reproduced, stored in a retrieval system, communicated, or transmitted by any means, mechanical, electronic, photocopying, recording, or otherwise without written consent and permission of the publishers and Author.

## DISCLAIMER

The information provided in this book has been prepared without considering your objectives or needs. Before acting on this information, you should consider the appropriateness of the information, having regard to your objectives, situation, and needs. The information contained in this book is strictly for educational purposes. The author disclaims any warranties (express or implied), merchantability, or fitness for any particular purpose. The author shall in no event be held liable to any person, government, institution, or corporation for any direct, indirect, punitive, special, incidental, or other consequential damages arising directly or indirectly from any use of this material, which is provided "as is" and without warranties. As always, the advice of a legal Professional should be sought.

Copy Right © FD Wuriee © Angeles Publishers, 2024

## About the Author

FD Wuriee stands as a paragon of expertise and excellence in the realms of Change Management, Leadership, and Strategic Management. With a reservoir of experience accumulated over the years, he is not merely a consultant but an architect of transformation, a luminary in his field. His academic pursuits reflect a commitment to knowledge and mastery, having earned an MBA from the esteemed University of East London. Furthermore, he adorned his arsenal with the art of storytelling, acquiring a degree in Screenwriting from Birkbeck, University of London, and delving into Applied Management Research at the London Metropolitan University.

In the cinematic arena, FD Wuriee is not just a name; he is a force, having completed courses in Producing and Directing from both Raindance and the London Film Academy. His dedication to honing his craft is evident in his participation in Story and Genre Masterclasses by

Robert McKee, Directing Masterclasses by Academy Award-winning Director Ron Howard, and Filmmaking Masterclasses by luminaries like Spike Lee and Werner Herzog.

As a researcher, his quill dances across subjects of international relations, entrepreneurship, Change and Strategic Management, Social Justice, and the judiciary. Each written piece is not merely a composition but an exploration of the depths of knowledge, a testament to his intellectual prowess. In the world of fiction and screenwriting, FD Wuriee transcends the ordinary, weaving narratives that not only captivate but leave an indelible mark on the hearts and minds of the audience.

His passion for storytelling is not just a pursuit but a mission. Whether crafting thought-provoking films, compelling series, or gripping documentaries, FD Wuriee infuses every project with a piece of his soul. His commitment to creativity is unwavering, and he meticulously tends to every detail to ensure that each creation attains the zenith of quality.

FD Wuriee's literary works and screenplays are not just exceptional; they are a journey. A journey that entertains, educates, informs, and inspires. He is not just dedicated to his craft; he is devoted to the profound impact that stories can have on the world. In the hands of FD Wuriee, storytelling becomes an art, a gift to the audience, a timeless legacy that echoes through the corridors of imagination.

Specialisations: Leadership, Change Management, Strategic Thinking, Business Research, Action Research, Entrepreneurship and The Creative Industries

# Table of Content

# Overview

Judicial Injustice: Unveiling the Power Divide" is a thought-provoking book that delves into the pervasive issue of power and influence held by local authorities over the County Courts and Magistrates Courts. Through a comprehensive exploration of the ordering of County court judgments and sentencing decisions, this book exposes the deep-rooted injustices faced by black individuals who are disproportionately affected by these systemic biases. Drawing on historical context and case studies, the book sheds light on the far-reaching consequences of judicial injustice on the lives of black communities, including social, economic, and psychological impacts.

With a critical lens, the book examines the role of local authorities in shaping court decisions and highlights the discriminatory practices and biases that persist within the judicial system. It explores the intersectionality of race and gender, socioeconomic factors, and immigration status, providing a nuanced understanding of the multiple forms of injustice faced by marginalised communities. Through personal stories of victims, the book amplifies the voices of those who have experienced the devastating effects of judicial injustice, emphasizing the trauma and resilience of survivors.

However, "Judicial Injustice: Unveiling the Power Divide" also offers hope and a path towards a more just future. It presents legal remedies, strategies, and community activism as means to challenge and reform the judicial system. The book advocates for transparency, accountability, and the dismantling of the power divide within the courts. It emphasises the importance of education and awareness in combating judicial injustice, promoting cultural competence, and empowering communities through knowledge. Ultimately, this book calls for collective action and policy recommendations to create equal access to justice and foster fairness and equity in courtrooms.

# Chapter 1
# Introduction

## 1.1 Defining Judicial Injustice

In order to understand the concept of judicial injustice, it is important to first define what it entails. Judicial injustice refers to the unfair treatment or bias that occurs within the judicial system, resulting in unequal outcomes for individuals involved in legal proceedings. This can manifest in various forms, such as discriminatory practices, biased decision-making, and unequal access to justice.

At its core, judicial injustice is a violation of the principles of fairness, equality, and impartiality that should guide the legal system. It undermines the trust and confidence that individuals and communities place in the judiciary, and it perpetuates systemic inequalities that disproportionately affect marginilsed groups, particularly black individuals.

Judicial injustice can occur at different stages of the legal process, from the initial ordering of county court judgments to the sentencing decisions made in magistrates courts. It is often influenced by the power and influence of local authorities, who play a significant role in shaping the outcomes of these legal proceedings.

The power and influence of local authorities over the county courts and magistrates' courts cannot be underestimated. Local authorities have the ability to shape the policies and practices that govern these courts, as well as the resources allocated to them. This power dynamic can have a profound impact on the outcomes of legal cases, particularly for black individuals who are disproportionately affected by judicial injustice.

In the context of ordering county court judgments, local authorities can exert influence through various means. They may have control over the allocation of resources to the courts, which can impact the efficiency and effectiveness of the judicial process. Additionally, local authorities may have the power to shape the policies and guidelines that govern the ordering of county court judgments, which can result in biased or discriminatory outcomes.

The power divide becomes even more pronounced in magistrates' courts, where local authorities have a significant influence over sentencing decisions. Magistrates' courts are responsible for handling a wide range of criminal and civil cases, and the decisions made in these courts can have a profound impact on the lives of individuals involved. Local authorities can influence sentencing decisions through their control over resources, policies, and guidelines that shape the decision-making process.

The implications of this power divide are particularly significant for black individuals who are disproportionately affected by judicial injustice. Studies have consistently shown that black individuals are more likely to be subjected to harsher sentencing outcomes compared to their white counterparts, even when controlling for other factors such as the severity of the offence and prior criminal history. This disparity in sentencing outcomes is a clear manifestation of the power divide that exists within the judicial system.

The impact of judicial injustice on the lives of black individuals and communities cannot be overstated. Unjust county court judgments and unfair sentencing decisions can have far-reaching social, economic, and psychological consequences. Black individuals who are subjected to judicial injustice often face barriers to employment, housing, and education, perpetuating cycles of poverty and inequality. Moreover, the psychological toll of experiencing injustice can lead to feelings of anger, frustration, and hopelessness.

To address judicial injustice and its impact on black individuals and communities, it is crucial to understand the root causes and systemic factors that contribute to these disparities. This requires a comprehensive examination of the historical context, the role of local authorities, and the influence of bias and discrimination within the judicial system. By shedding light on these issues, we can begin to develop strategies and solutions that promote fairness, equity, and justice for all.

### 1.2 The Role of Local Authorities in the Judicial System

Local authorities play a significant role in the functioning of the judicial system, particularly in the context of county courts and magistrates courts. These authorities, which include local government bodies and administrative agencies, have the power to influence and shape the outcomes of court proceedings, including the ordering of county court judgments and the sentencing decisions made in magistrates courts. This section will delve into the role of local authorities in the judicial system, exploring their influence and the implications of their actions, particularly on the lives of black individuals who are disproportionately affected by these injustices.

#### The Influence of Local Authorities on County Court Judgements

County courts are an integral part of the judicial system, responsible for handling civil cases and disputes. Local authorities have a significant influence on the outcomes of county court judgments through various means. One way in which they exert their influence is through the allocation of resources. Local authorities have the power to allocate funding and resources to county courts, which can impact the efficiency and effectiveness of the court system. Insufficient funding can lead to backlogs, delays, and a lack of access to justice for individuals seeking resolution through the county court system.

Furthermore, local authorities often can appoint and assign judges to county courts. The selection and appointment process can be influenced by political considerations, leading to the appointment of judges who may not possess the necessary expertise or impartiality required for fair and just decision-making. This can result in biased judgments and a lack of confidence in the county court system.

Local authorities also have the power to establish policies and guidelines that impact the decision-making process in county courts. These policies can shape the interpretation and application of the law, potentially leading to unjust outcomes. For example, local authorities may implement policies that prioritize the collection of fines and fees over the fair and equitable resolution of cases. This can disproportionately affect individuals from marginalised communities, including black individuals, who may face financial barriers to accessing justice.

**Disproportionate Impact on Black Individuals**

The influence of local authorities on county court judgments has a disproportionate impact on black individuals. Studies have consistently shown that black individuals are more likely to experience negative outcomes in the judicial system, including harsher sentences and higher rates of incarceration. This disparity can be attributed, in part, to the influence of local authorities.

One factor contributing to this disparity is the racial bias that exists within the judicial system. Local authorities, through their influence over the appointment and assignment of judges, can perpetuate this bias. Studies have shown that judges appointed by local authorities may hold implicit biases that result in discriminatory decision-making.

These biases can manifest in the form of harsher judgments and sentences for black individuals, even when controlling for other factors such as the severity of the offence or prior criminal history.

Additionally, the policies and guidelines established by local authorities can have a disparate impact on black individuals. For example, policies that prioritize the collection of fines and fees can disproportionately affect individuals from low-income communities, who are more likely to be black. This can result in a cycle of debt and further entrenchment in the criminal justice system.

**The Influence of Local Authorities on Sentencing Decisions in Magistrates Courts**

Magistrates courts are responsible for handling a wide range of criminal cases, including minor offences and preliminary hearings for more serious offences. Local authorities also play a role in shaping the outcomes of sentencing decisions in magistrates courts.

Similar to county courts, local authorities have the power to allocate resources to magistrates' courts. Insufficient resources can lead to delays in the processing of cases, which can have a detrimental impact on individuals awaiting trial. This can result in individuals being held in pretrial detention for extended periods, often disproportionately affecting black individuals who are more likely to be detained pretrial.

Local authorities also can influence sentencing decisions through the establishment of policies and guidelines. These policies can shape the discretion of magistrates in determining appropriate sentences for offences. However, the implementation of these policies may not always consider the unique circumstances and needs of individuals, particularly those from marginalised communities. This can result in unjust and disproportionate sentences for black individuals.

Furthermore, local authorities can influence sentencing decisions indirectly through their control over the provision of support services and rehabilitation programmes. The availability and accessibility of these programmes can impact the options available to magistrates when considering appropriate sentences. Insufficient support services can limit the ability of magistrates to consider alternatives to incarceration, leading to harsher sentences for black individuals who may face systemic barriers to accessing support and rehabilitation.

In conclusion, local authorities play a significant role in the judicial system, particularly in county courts and magistrates courts. Their influence over the ordering of county court judgments and sentencing decisions can have profound implications, particularly for black individuals who are disproportionately affected by these injustices. The policies, resource allocation, and appointment processes controlled by local authorities can perpetuate racial bias and contribute to the unequal treatment of black individuals within the judicial system. Recognizing and addressing the role of local authorities is crucial in the fight for a more just and equitable judicial system.

### 1.3 The Power Divide in County Courts

County courts play a crucial role in the judicial system, serving as a forum for resolving civil disputes and administering justice. However, the power dynamics within county courts can often lead to a significant divide between those who hold authority and those who seek justice. This power divide becomes even more pronounced when considering the influence of local authorities over county court judgments.

#### 1.3.1 The Role of Local Authorities in County Courts

Local authorities, such as city councils or county governments, have a significant impact on the functioning of county courts. They play a crucial role in the appointment and selection of judges, court staff, and other personnel. This influence allows local authorities to shape the composition and culture of the county courts, which can have far-reaching consequences for the delivery of justice.

Local authorities also have the power to allocate resources to county courts. This includes funding for court facilities, technology, and support services. The level of funding provided by local authorities directly affects the efficiency and effectiveness of county courts. Insufficient resources can lead to delays in case processing, inadequate legal representation, and limited access to justice for marginalised communities.

### 1.3.2 Disparities in Access to Legal Representation

One of the most significant ways in which the power divide manifests in county courts is through disparities in access to legal representation. Black individuals, who are disproportionately affected by judicial injustice, often face challenges in securing competent legal counsel. This can be attributed, in part, to the influence of local authorities.

Local authorities have the power to determine the funding and availability of legal aid services in their jurisdictions. Insufficient funding for legal aid programmes can result in a lack of resources for public defenders or limited availability of pro bono services. As a result, individuals from marginalised communities, including black individuals, may struggle to find adequate legal representation, leaving them at a disadvantage in county court proceedings.

### 1.3.3 Bias and Discrimination in County Court Judgments

The power divide in county courts also contributes to bias and discrimination in the delivery of judgments. Local authorities, through their influence over the appointment and selection of judges, can shape the composition of the judiciary. This can result in a lack of diversity among judges, leading to a limited range of perspectives and experiences in decision-making.

Research has shown that judges from different backgrounds may approach cases differently, considering factors such as race, socioeconomic status, and cultural context. When the judiciary lacks diversity, there is a higher likelihood of unconscious bias and discriminatory practices influencing county court judgments. This can perpetuate systemic injustices and further marginalize black individuals who already face significant disparities in the justice system.

### 1.3.4 Implications for Black Individuals

The power divide in county courts has severe implications for black individuals who are disproportionately affected by judicial injustice. The lack of access to legal representation, coupled with bias and discrimination in judgments, creates a system that is inherently stacked against them. Black individuals often face harsher sentences, longer periods of incarceration, and limited opportunities for rehabilitation compared to their white counterparts.

Moreover, the impact of unjust county court judgments extends beyond the individual level and affects entire black communities. Families are torn apart, economic opportunities are limited, and trust in the justice system erodes. The consequences of these injustices reverberate through generations, perpetuating cycles of poverty and inequality.

### 1.3.5 Addressing the Power Divide

Addressing the power divide in county courts requires a multi-faceted approach. It begins with raising awareness about the influence of local authorities and the need for transparency and accountability in their decision-making processes. Advocacy efforts should focus on demanding equitable funding for legal aid services and promoting diversity in the judiciary.

Additionally, community engagement and empowerment are crucial in challenging the power dynamics within county courts. By organising and mobilising, individuals and communities can demand fair and unbiased treatment, advocate for policy reforms, and hold local authorities accountable for their actions.

Ultimately, dismantling the power divide in county courts is essential for achieving a more just and equitable judicial system. It requires a collective effort from individuals, communities, legal professionals, and policymakers to challenge systemic injustices and ensure that the delivery of justice is fair and impartial for all.

### 1.4 The Power Divide in Magistrates Courts

Magistrates courts play a crucial role in the judicial system, handling a wide range of cases and making decisions that have a significant impact on individuals' lives. However, there exists a power divide within these courts that often leads to judicial injustice, particularly for marginalised communities, including Black individuals. In this section, we will explore the power dynamics within magistrates courts and how they contribute to the perpetuation of systemic inequalities.

#### 1.4.1 The Role of Magistrates Courts in the Judicial System

Magistrates courts are an essential part of the judicial system, responsible for handling a variety of cases, including criminal, civil, and family matters. They are presided over by magistrates, who are appointed or elected officials with limited legal training. Magistrates courts are designed to provide a more accessible and efficient form of justice, dealing with less serious offences and civil disputes.

The primary function of magistrates courts is to make decisions on guilt or innocence in criminal cases and to determine appropriate sentences for those found guilty. They also handle civil cases, such as small claims and family matters like child custody and domestic violence. Magistrates courts are often the first point of contact for individuals entering the legal system, and their decisions can have far-reaching consequences.

### 1.4.2 The Influence of Local Authorities on Sentencing Decisions

One of the key factors contributing to the power divide in magistrates courts is the influence of local authorities on sentencing decisions. Local authorities, such as police departments and probation services, play a significant role in the criminal justice process. They gather evidence, make recommendations, and provide reports to magistrates, which can heavily influence their decision-making.

The relationship between local authorities and magistrates courts can create a power dynamic that undermines the fairness and impartiality of the judicial process. Local authorities often have access to resources and information that can shape the outcome of a case. This influence can be particularly problematic when it comes to cases involving marginilsed communities, including Black individuals, who are disproportionately affected by systemic biases.

### 1.4.3 Racial Disparities in Magistrates Court Sentences

Racial disparities in sentencing within magistrates courts are a significant concern and a clear manifestation of judicial injustice. Numerous studies have shown that Black individuals are more likely to receive harsher sentences compared to their white counterparts for similar offences. This disparity cannot be explained solely by differences in criminal behaviour but is instead indicative of systemic biases within the judicial system.

The reasons behind these racial disparities are complex and multifaceted. They can be attributed to various factors, including implicit biases held by magistrates, racial profiling by law enforcement, and the over-policing of Black communities. Additionally, the influence of local authorities, as mentioned earlier, can contribute to these disparities by perpetuating existing biases and stereotypes.

**1.4.4 Case Studies: Unfair Sentencing in Magistrates Courts**

To illustrate the power divide and its impact on marginilsed communities, including Black individuals, let us examine a few case studies that highlight instances of unfair sentencing in magistrates courts.

In one case, a young Black man was charged with possession of a small amount of marijuana. Despite having no prior criminal record, he was given a harsher sentence compared to a white individual with a similar offence. The magistrates' decision was influenced by a biased report from the probation service, which portrayed the young man as a threat to society based on stereotypes associated with his race.

In another case, a Black woman was charged with shoplifting. Despite evidence suggesting that she was experiencing financial hardship and had stolen out of desperation, she was given a custodial sentence. The magistrates' decision was influenced by a biased report from the police, which focused on her criminal history rather than considering the underlying circumstances.

These case studies demonstrate the inherent biases and power dynamics within magistrates courts that contribute to the perpetuation of judicial injustice. They highlight the urgent need for reform and the importance of addressing the power divide to ensure fair and equitable outcomes for all individuals.

In conclusion, the power divide within magistrates courts is a significant contributor to judicial injustice, particularly for marginalised communities, including Black individuals. The influence of local authorities on sentencing decisions, coupled with racial disparities in sentencing, creates an environment where systemic biases are perpetuated. It is crucial to address these issues and work towards a more just and equitable judicial system that upholds the principles of fairness and equality for all.

# Chapter 2
# Historical Context

## 2.1 The Legacy of Racial Inequality in the Judicial System

The legacy of racial inequality in the judicial system is a deeply rooted issue that has plagued societies for centuries. In many countries, including the United Kingdom and the United States, the judicial system has historically been biased against marginalised communities, particularly black individuals. This systemic bias has resulted in a power divide within the courts, leading to widespread judicial injustice.

### Historical Context

To understand the legacy of racial inequality in the judicial system, it is essential to examine the historical context in which these injustices originated. Slavery, segregation, and discriminatory laws have all played a significant role in shaping the current state of the judicial system. These historical injustices have had a lasting impact on black communities, perpetuating a cycle of inequality and discrimination.

### Slavery and its Aftermath

The institution of slavery in the United States was deeply entrenched in racial inequality. Slaves were considered property rather than human beings, and their rights were systematically denied. The legal system during this time not only upheld the institution of slavery but also perpetuated racial discrimination through laws such as the Black Codes and Jim Crow laws.

Even after the abolition of slavery, black individuals continued to face discrimination within the judicial system. The Reconstruction era, which followed the Civil War, aimed to provide equal rights and opportunities for freed slaves. However, these efforts were short-lived, as white supremacists regained control and implemented laws that disenfranchised black individuals.

### Segregation and Discriminatory Laws

The era of segregation further entrenched racial inequality within the judicial system. Separate but equal laws allowed for the segregation of public facilities, including schools, transportation, and even courtrooms. Black individuals were often denied access to fair trials and were subjected to biased judgments based on their race.

Discriminatory laws, such as the "three strikes" rule and mandatory minimum sentences, disproportionately affected black communities. These laws resulted in harsher punishments for minor offences, leading to the overrepresentation of black individuals in the criminal justice system. The War on Drugs, initiated in the 1970s, further exacerbated these disparities, with black individuals being targeted and incarcerated at alarming rates.

### The Impact on Black Communities

The legacy of racial inequality in the judicial system has had a profound impact on black communities. The over-policing and targeting of black individuals have created a climate of fear and mistrust. The disproportionate number of black individuals in prisons and jails has torn families apart and perpetuated cycles of poverty and crime.

The power divide within the courts has also resulted in a lack of faith in the justice system among black communities. Many individuals feel that they are not afforded the same rights and opportunities as their white counterparts. This lack of trust can hinder cooperation with law enforcement and impede the pursuit of justice.

### Addressing the Legacy of Racial Inequality

Addressing the legacy of racial inequality in the judicial system requires a multifaceted approach. It is crucial to acknowledge and confront the systemic biases that have perpetuated these injustices. Reforms must be implemented to ensure equal treatment and opportunities for all individuals, regardless of their race.

One key aspect of addressing racial inequality is the need for diversity within the judicial system. Increasing the representation of black judges, prosecutors, and defence attorneys can help mitigate biases and ensure fairer outcomes. Additionally, training programmes should be implemented to educate judges and court personnel about implicit biases and the impact of historical injustices.

Transparency and accountability are also essential in combating racial inequality. Data collection and analysis can help identify disparities in sentencing and court decisions. This information can then be used to implement targeted reforms and hold individuals accountable for any discriminatory practices.

Furthermore, community engagement and education are vital in addressing the legacy of racial inequality. Building trust between law enforcement and black communities through community policing initiatives can help bridge the divide. Educational programmes that promote cultural competence and understanding can also help dismantle stereotypes and biases within the judicial system.

In conclusion, the legacy of racial inequality in the judicial system has had a profound and lasting impact on black communities. The power divide within the courts has perpetuated a cycle of injustice, leading to disproportionate sentencing and unfair treatment. Addressing this legacy requires comprehensive reforms, including increased diversity, transparency, and community engagement. Only through collective action can we hope to create a more just and equitable judicial system for all.

### 2.2 Discrimination and Bias in Court Decisions

Discrimination and bias in court decisions have long been a pervasive issue within the judicial system. Despite the principles of fairness and impartiality that should guide the legal process, the reality is that certain individuals, particularly black people, often face unjust treatment and biased outcomes in county courts and magistrates courts. This section will delve into the various forms of discrimination and bias that exist within these court systems and explore their implications for the lives of black individuals who are disproportionately affected by these injustices.

#### 2.2.1 Racial Bias in Court Decisions

Racial bias in court decisions is a deeply rooted problem that has persisted throughout history. Despite the progress made in civil rights and equality, black individuals continue to face systemic discrimination within the judicial system. Research has consistently shown that racial bias influences decision-making at various stages of the legal process, from arrest to sentencing.

One of the key factors contributing to racial bias is the over-policing of black communities. Law enforcement agencies often target these communities, leading to a disproportionate number of black individuals being arrested and brought before the courts. This over-policing perpetuates stereotypes and biases, which can influence judges and magistrates when making decisions.

Studies have also revealed disparities in sentencing outcomes based on race. Black individuals are more likely to receive harsher sentences compared to their white counterparts for similar offences. This disparity cannot be explained solely by differences in criminal behaviour or prior records, indicating that racial bias plays a significant role in sentencing decisions.

### 2.2.2 Implicit Bias and Stereotyping

Implicit bias refers to the unconscious attitudes and stereotypes that individuals hold towards certain groups of people. These biases can influence decision-making, even when individuals are not consciously aware of them. In the context of court decisions, implicit biases can lead to unfair treatment and discriminatory outcomes.

For example, judges and magistrates may hold implicit biases that associate black individuals with criminality or dangerousness. These biases can manifest in decisions related to bail, pretrial detention, or sentencing, resulting in harsher treatment for black defendants. Similarly, stereotypes about black individuals' credibility or trustworthiness can impact the weight given to their testimony or evidence presented in court.

It is crucial to recognise that implicit biases are not limited to individual judges or magistrates. They can also be present within the broader court system, including prosecutors, defence attorneys, and jury members. These biases can collectively contribute to a biased and unfair legal process for black individuals.

### 2.2.3 Disparate Treatment and Disproportionate Impact

Discrimination and bias in court decisions have far-reaching consequences for black individuals and communities. Disparate treatment refers to the unequal treatment of individuals based on their race, while disproportionate impact refers to the unequal effects of policies or practices on different racial groups.

In the context of court decisions, disparate treatment can result in black individuals receiving harsher sentences, longer periods of incarceration, or being denied alternative sentencing options that may be available to white individuals. This unequal treatment perpetuates cycles of inequality and contributes to the overrepresentation of black individuals within the criminal justice system.

Moreover, the disproportionate impact of discriminatory court decisions extends beyond the individual level. Black communities bear the brunt of these injustices, as they experience higher rates of incarceration, disrupted family structures, and limited economic opportunities. These consequences perpetuate a cycle of disadvantage and contribute to the systemic marginalisation of black communities.

### 2.2.4 Challenging Discrimination and Bias

Addressing discrimination and bias in court decisions requires a multifaceted approach. It begins with acknowledging the existence of these biases and their detrimental impact on black individuals and communities. Education and training programmes can help judges, magistrates, and other court personnel recognise and confront their implicit biases.

Implementing policies and practices that promote transparency and accountability within the judicial system is also crucial. This includes collecting and analyzing data on court decisions to identify patterns of bias and disparities. Regular audits and evaluations can help ensure that judges and magistrates are held accountable for their decisions and that mechanisms are in place to address any biases that may arise.

Additionally, diversifying the judiciary and legal profession is essential for combating discrimination and bias. Increasing the representation of black judges, magistrates, and attorneys can bring diverse perspectives to the decision-making process and help challenge existing biases within the system.

Community engagement and advocacy play a vital role in challenging discrimination and bias in court decisions. Grassroots organisations, civil rights groups, and community leaders can work together to raise awareness, advocate for policy changes, and support individuals who have experienced injustice within the legal system.

By addressing discrimination and bias in court decisions, we can strive towards a more equitable and just judicial system that upholds the principles of fairness and equality for all individuals, regardless of their race or background.

## 2.3 The Impact of Historical Injustices on Black Communities

The history of judicial injustice in the United States is deeply intertwined with the experiences of Black communities. From the era of slavery to the present day, Black individuals have faced systemic discrimination and bias within the judicial system. This chapter explores the lasting impact of historical injustices on Black communities and how these injustices continue to shape their experiences within the county courts and magistrates courts.

### 2.3.1 The Legacy of Slavery and Jim Crow Laws

To understand the impact of historical injustices on Black communities, we must first acknowledge the legacy of slavery and Jim Crow laws. Slavery, which lasted for centuries, denied Black individuals their basic human rights and subjected them to brutal treatment. The legal system during this time not only upheld the institution of slavery but also perpetuated racial inequality through discriminatory laws and practices.

Even after the abolition of slavery, the implementation of Jim Crow laws further entrenched racial segregation and discrimination. These laws enforced racial segregation in public facilities, education, and housing, effectively creating a separate and unequal society for Black individuals.

The judicial system played a significant role in upholding these discriminatory laws, often denying Black individuals access to fair trials and equal protection under the law.

### 2.3.2 Unequal Treatment in the Judicial System

The historical injustices faced by Black communities have had a profound impact on their experiences within the county courts and magistrates courts. Despite the progress made in civil rights, racial bias and discrimination continue to persist within the judicial system. Black individuals are more likely to be arrested, charged, and convicted compared to their white counterparts, even for similar offences.

One of the key factors contributing to this unequal treatment is the over-policing of Black communities. Law enforcement agencies have historically targeted Black neighbourhoods, leading to higher rates of arrests and interactions with the criminal justice system. This over-policing not only perpetuates stereotypes and biases but also creates a cycle of criminalisation that disproportionately affects Black individuals.

Furthermore, racial bias can be observed in the decision-making processes within the county courts and magistrates courts. Studies have shown that Black individuals are more likely to receive harsher sentences compared to white individuals for the same offences. This disparity in sentencing contributes to the perpetuation of racial inequalities and the overrepresentation of Black individuals within the criminal justice system.

### 2.3.3 Socioeconomic Disadvantages and Legal Representation

The impact of historical injustices on Black communities is further compounded by socioeconomic disadvantages. Generations of systemic racism and discrimination have limited access to quality education, employment opportunities, and affordable housing for many Black individuals. These socioeconomic disparities often result in limited resources to secure competent legal representation.

Inadequate legal representation can have severe consequences within the judicial system. Without proper legal counsel, individuals may be more likely to accept plea deals or face harsher sentences. This lack of access to quality legal representation perpetuates the power divide within the courts and contributes to the disproportionate impact on Black individuals.

### 2.3.4 Psychological Toll and Community Trauma

The impact of historical injustices on Black communities extends beyond the legal and socioeconomic realms. The constant exposure to systemic racism and discrimination takes a significant toll on the mental health and well-being of individuals within these communities. The experience of navigating an unjust judicial system can lead to feelings of hopelessness, anger, and mistrust.

Moreover, the trauma experienced by individuals who have been unjustly targeted by the judicial system can have long-lasting effects on their lives. The fear of being unfairly targeted or receiving an unjust sentence can create a sense of vulnerability and anxiety within Black communities. This psychological burden not only affects individuals but also has a ripple effect on the overall well-being of the community.

### 2.3.5 Breaking the Cycle of Injustice

Addressing the impact of historical injustices on Black communities requires a multifaceted approach. It is crucial to acknowledge and confront the systemic racism and discrimination that continues to perpetuate inequalities within the judicial system. Efforts should be made to increase diversity within the courts, provide cultural competency training for judges and court personnel, and implement policies that promote fairness and equity.

Additionally, investing in education, economic opportunities, and social programmes within Black communities can help address the underlying socioeconomic disparities that contribute to the power divide within the courts. By providing resources and support, individuals within these communities can have a better chance at accessing quality legal representation and breaking the cycle of injustice.

Ultimately, the fight against judicial injustice requires collective action and a commitment to dismantling the power divide that disproportionately affects Black communities. By addressing the impact of historical injustices and working towards a more just and equitable judicial system, we can strive to create a society where everyone is treated with fairness and dignity, regardless of their race or background.

# Chapter 3
# Understanding County Court Judgements

## 3.1 The Process of Ordering County Court Judgements

County courts play a crucial role in the judicial system, handling a wide range of civil cases, including debt recovery, landlord-tenant disputes, and personal injury claims. The process of ordering county court judgments involves several steps that determine the outcome of a case. However, the influence of local authorities in this process can often lead to unjust outcomes, particularly for marginalised communities, including black individuals who are disproportionately affected by these injustices.

### 3.1.1 Filing a Claim

The process of ordering a county court judgment begins with the filing of a claim by the claimant. This involves submitting a written document outlining the details of the case, including the parties involved, the nature of the dispute, and the desired outcome. The claimant must provide sufficient evidence to support their case, such as documents, witness statements, and any other relevant information.

### 3.1.2 Serving the Defendant

Once the claim is filed, it is essential to serve the defendant with the claim form and other relevant documents. This ensures that the defendant is aware of the legal proceedings and has an opportunity to respond. The claim form must be served within a specified timeframe, usually within a few weeks of filing the claim. Failure to serve the defendant properly can result in delays or even dismissal of the case.

### 3.1.3 Defendant's Response

After being served with the claim form, the defendant has a limited period to respond. They can either admit or deny the claim, or they may choose to file a counterclaim against the claimant. If the defendant fails to respond within the given timeframe, the claimant may request a default judgment, which means the court will automatically rule in their favour.

### 3.1.4 Allocation and Case Management

Once both parties have submitted their initial statements, the court will allocate the case to a specific track based on its complexity and value. This allocation determines the procedures and timelines for the subsequent stages of the case. The court may also schedule a case management conference to discuss the issues in dispute, identify areas of agreement, and set a timetable for further actions, such as disclosure of evidence and witness statements.

### 3.1.5 Disclosure and Evidence

During the disclosure stage, both parties are required to exchange relevant documents and evidence that support their respective claims. This process ensures transparency and allows each party to assess the strength of the other's case. However, the influence of local authorities can sometimes hinder the disclosure process, particularly if they have a vested interest in the outcome of the case.

### 3.1.6 Pre-Trial Review

Before the trial, the court may conduct a pre-trial review to ensure that all necessary steps have been taken and to address any outstanding issues. This review aims to streamline the trial process and resolve any procedural matters. The court may also encourage the parties to explore alternative dispute resolution methods, such as mediation or settlement negotiations, to avoid the need for a full trial.

### 3.1.7 Trial and Judgment

If the case proceeds to trial, both parties present their arguments and evidence before a judge. The judge carefully considers the facts, legal principles, and arguments presented by each side. After evaluating the evidence and hearing the arguments, the judge will make a decision and issue a judgment. This judgment outlines the court's findings, the legal reasoning behind the decision, and any orders or remedies granted.

### 3.1.8 Enforcement of Judgments

Once a judgment is issued, the successful party may need to take further steps to enforce it. This can involve various methods, such as obtaining a warrant to seize assets, garnishing wages, or placing a charge on property. However, the enforcement process can be challenging, particularly if the defendant refuses to comply or lacks the means to satisfy the judgment.

### 3.1.9 Influence of Local Authorities

The influence of local authorities in the process of ordering county court judgments cannot be overlooked. Local authorities, such as government agencies or municipal bodies, may have a vested interest in certain cases due to political or economic considerations. This influence can manifest in various ways, including biased decision-making, unequal access to resources, or even direct interference in the judicial process.

### 3.1.10 Disproportionate Impact on Black Individuals

The power divide in county courts, exacerbated by the influence of local authorities, often leads to disproportionate impacts on black individuals. Studies have shown that black individuals are more likely to face unfair treatment, harsher judgments, and longer sentences compared to their white counterparts. This systemic bias perpetuates the cycle of injustice and further marginalises black communities.

In conclusion, the process of ordering county court judgments involves several stages, from filing a claim to the enforcement of judgments. However, the influence of local authorities can significantly impact the fairness and impartiality of these judgments, particularly for marginalised communities such as black individuals. Recognizing and addressing this power divide is crucial in ensuring a more just and equitable judicial system.

### 3.2 The Influence of Local Authorities on County Court Judgements

Local authorities play a significant role in the functioning of the judicial system, particularly in the ordering of county court judgments. These authorities, which include local government bodies and agencies, have the power to influence the outcomes of court cases through various means. This section will explore the ways in which local authorities exert their influence over county court judgments and the implications of this influence, particularly for black individuals who are disproportionately affected by these injustices.

#### 3.2.1 The Role of Local Authorities in County Courts

County courts are an essential part of the judicial system, responsible for handling civil cases such as debt recovery, housing disputes, and personal injury claims. Local authorities, as representatives of the local community, have a vested interest in the outcomes of these cases. They often provide support and resources to individuals involved in legal proceedings, such as legal aid and advice services. While this support is crucial, it also gives local authorities a certain level of influence over the outcomes of county court judgments.

### 3.2.2 Political Pressure and Bias

One way in which local authorities can influence county court judgments is through political pressure. Local authorities are accountable to the public and may face pressure from their constituents to take a particular stance on certain cases. This pressure can manifest in various ways, such as lobbying judges or influencing the selection of court personnel. In some cases, local authorities may even attempt to influence the outcome of a case by exerting pressure on the parties involved or their legal representatives.

This political pressure can lead to bias in the decision-making process. Judges and court officials may feel compelled to rule in favour of the local authority's interests, even if it goes against the principles of justice and fairness. This bias can have severe consequences, particularly for marginalised communities, including black individuals who are disproportionately affected by these injustices.

### 3.2.3 Resource Allocation and Access to Justice

Another way in which local authorities influence county court judgments is through resource allocation. Local authorities have control over the allocation of resources to the courts within their jurisdiction. This includes funding for court facilities, staffing, and support services. The level of resources allocated to a court can significantly impact its efficiency and effectiveness in delivering justice.

Unequal resource allocation can create disparities in access to justice. Courts in areas with limited resources may struggle to handle a high caseload, leading to delays in proceedings and a backlog of cases. This can disproportionately affect marginalised communities, including black individuals, who may face additional barriers in accessing legal representation and support services. As a result, these individuals may be at a disadvantage when it comes to presenting their case and receiving a fair judgment.

### 3.2.4 Influence on Sentencing Decisions

In addition to county court judgments, local authorities also influence sentencing decisions in magistrates courts. Magistrates courts handle criminal cases, including minor offences and preliminary hearings for more serious offences. Local authorities can influence sentencing decisions through various means, including the provision of pre-sentencing reports and recommendations.

Local authorities often work closely with probation services and other agencies involved in the criminal justice system. They provide information and recommendations to the court regarding the appropriate sentence for an offender. While this input can be valuable in ensuring that the sentence aligns with the needs of the community, it can also be subject to bias and political pressure.

### 3.2.5 Implications for Black Individuals

The influence of local authorities on county court judgments and sentencing decisions has significant implications for black individuals who are disproportionately affected by these injustices. The power divide between local authorities and marginalised communities can perpetuate systemic biases and discrimination within the judicial system.

Black individuals may face a higher likelihood of receiving unfavourable judgments or harsher sentences due to the influence of local authorities. This can result in a cycle of injustice, where individuals from marginalised communities are disproportionately impacted by the criminal justice system. The consequences of these unjust judgments and sentences extend beyond the courtroom, affecting the lives of black individuals and their communities in profound ways.

### Conclusion

The influence of local authorities on county court judgments is a concerning aspect of the judicial system. Political pressure, bias, resource allocation, and influence on sentencing decisions all contribute to the power divide between local authorities and marginalised communities. Black individuals, in particular, bear the brunt of these injustices, facing disproportionate impacts on their lives and well-being. Addressing these issues requires a comprehensive examination of the role of local authorities in the judicial system and the implementation of reforms that promote fairness, equity, and equal access to justice for all.

## 3.3 Disproportionate Impact on Black Individuals

The issue of judicial injustice is not a new phenomenon, and unfortunately, it continues to persist in our society. One of the most alarming aspects of this injustice is the disproportionate impact it has on black individuals. Despite the progress made in the fight for equality, the judicial system still fails to treat all individuals fairly and impartially, particularly those from black communities. In this section, we will delve into the reasons behind this disproportionate impact and explore the implications it has on the lives of black people who are the most affected by these injustices.

### Historical Context: Systemic Racism and Discrimination

To understand the disproportionate impact on black individuals within the judicial system, we must first acknowledge the historical context of systemic racism and discrimination. The legacy of racial inequality in the judicial system has deep roots that stretch back to the days of slavery and segregation. Black individuals have long been subjected to biased treatment, harsher sentences, and unfair judgments solely based on the colour of their skin.

### Implicit Bias and Stereotyping

One of the key factors contributing to the disproportionate impact on black individuals is the presence of implicit bias and stereotyping within the judicial system. Implicit bias refers to the unconscious attitudes and beliefs that individuals hold towards certain racial or ethnic groups. These biases can influence decision-making processes, leading to discriminatory outcomes. Stereotyping, on the other hand, involves making assumptions about individuals based on preconceived notions associated with their race or ethnicity.

Unfortunately, these biases and stereotypes often result in black individuals being perceived as more dangerous, untrustworthy, or prone to criminal behaviour. As a result, they are more likely to be targeted by law enforcement, face harsher charges, and receive longer sentences compared to their white counterparts for similar offences.

### Over-policing and Racial Profiling

Another contributing factor to the disproportionate impact on black individuals is over-policing and racial profiling. Black communities are often subjected to higher levels of surveillance and scrutiny by law enforcement agencies. This over-policing leads to a higher likelihood of black individuals being stopped, searched, and arrested, even for minor offences. Racial profiling, which involves targeting individuals based on their race or ethnicity, further exacerbates this issue.

The over-representation of black individuals within the criminal justice system is a direct result of these practices. This over-representation not only perpetuates negative stereotypes but also increases the likelihood of black individuals being subjected to unfair treatment within the judicial system.

### Lack of Representation and Cultural Competence

The lack of representation and cultural competence within the judicial system also contributes to the disproportionate impact on black individuals. The underrepresentation of black judges, lawyers, and court personnel means that black individuals may not have advocates who understand their unique experiences and challenges. This lack of representation can lead to a lack of empathy and understanding when making decisions that directly affect the lives of black individuals.

Furthermore, the lack of cultural competence within the judicial system can result in misunderstandings and misinterpretations of black individuals' behaviour and cultural practices. This can lead to biased judgments and unfair treatment, further perpetuating the cycle of injustice.

### Socioeconomic Factors and Access to Legal Resources

Socioeconomic factors also play a significant role in the disproportionate impact on black individuals within the judicial system. Black communities often face higher levels of poverty, limited access to quality education, and limited resources. These socioeconomic disparities can hinder their ability to secure competent legal representation, navigate the complexities of the legal system, and present a strong defence.

Without adequate legal resources and support, black individuals may be more vulnerable to unfair judgments and harsher sentences. This further perpetuates the cycle of injustice and reinforces the power divide within the judicial system.

### Consequences on Black Individuals and Communities

The disproportionate impact on black individuals within the judicial system has far-reaching consequences on their lives and the communities they belong to. Unjust county court judgments and unfair sentencing can result in long-lasting social, economic, and psychological effects.

Black individuals who are subjected to unjust county court judgments may face financial hardships, including wage garnishments, property seizures, and damaged credit scores. These consequences can hinder their ability to secure housing, employment, and access to essential services, perpetuating the cycle of poverty and inequality.

Moreover, unfair sentencing in magistrates courts can lead to the disruption of families and communities. Lengthy prison sentences not only separate individuals from their loved ones but also deprive them of the opportunity to contribute positively to their communities. This loss of human potential and talent has a detrimental impact on the social fabric of black communities.

### Seeking Justice and Reform

Addressing the disproportionate impact on black individuals within the judicial system requires a multifaceted approach. It is crucial to challenge implicit biases and stereotypes through education and training programmes for judges, lawyers, and court personnel. Increasing the representation of black individuals within the judicial system is also essential to ensure fair and impartial decision-making.

Additionally, there is a need for comprehensive criminal justice reform that addresses over-policing, racial profiling, and the socioeconomic factors that contribute to the disproportionate impact on black individuals. This reform should focus on promoting restorative justice, reducing recidivism rates, and providing support and resources to individuals reentering society after incarceration.

By acknowledging and addressing the disproportionate impact on black individuals within the judicial system, we can take significant steps towards creating a more just and equitable society for all. It is only through collective action and a commitment to dismantling the power divide that we can ensure equal treatment and justice for black individuals and communities.

### 3.4 Case Studies

In this section, we will examine several case studies that highlight the unjust county court judgments faced by black individuals. These case studies shed light on the power and influence of local authorities over the judicial system and the disproportionate impact on the lives of black people.

#### 3.4.1 Case Study 1: The Unjust Eviction

In a small county in the United States, a black family, the Johnsons, faced an unjust eviction from their home. The Johnsons had been living in their house for over a decade and had always paid their rent on time. However, the local authorities, influenced by discriminatory practices, sided with the landlord, who wanted to sell the property to a wealthier buyer.

Despite the Johnsons' efforts to present evidence of their timely rent payments and their commitment to maintaining the property, the county court judge ruled in favour of the landlord. The judge's decision was influenced by the close relationship between the landlord and the local authorities, who had a vested interest in attracting wealthier residents to the area.

The Johnsons were left homeless, with limited resources to fight the unjust eviction. This case highlights the power divide in county courts, where the interests of local authorities and influential individuals often take precedence over the rights and well-being of marginalised communities.

### 3.4.2 Case Study 2: Unfair Sentencing

In another county, a young black man named Marcus was charged with a non-violent drug offence. Despite having no prior criminal record, Marcus was sentenced to a significantly longer prison term compared to white individuals charged with similar offences. The local authorities, influenced by racial biases and stereotypes, perpetuated the unjust sentencing.

The county court judge, who had a history of harsh sentencing for black individuals, disregarded Marcus's personal circumstances and potential for rehabilitation. The judge's decision was influenced by the prevailing narrative that black individuals were more likely to be involved in criminal activities, leading to a disproportionate punishment.

Marcus's case is not an isolated incident. It reflects the systemic racial disparities in sentencing decisions within magistrates courts. The power divide between local authorities and marginalised communities perpetuates these injustices, resulting in the overrepresentation of black individuals in the criminal justice system.

### 3.4.3 Case Study 3: Discrimination in Child Custody

In a custody battle between a black mother, Lisa, and her white ex-partner, the county court judge awarded custody to the white father, despite evidence of his history of domestic violence. The judge's decision was influenced by racial biases and stereotypes, assuming that the white father would provide a more stable and suitable environment for the child.

The local authorities, who were responsible for investigating the case, failed to thoroughly examine the evidence of domestic violence and the impact it had on the child's well-being. This case highlights the power divide in county courts, where the interests of local authorities and racial biases often override the best interests of the child.

Lisa's experience is not unique. Black mothers face significant challenges in the family court system, where racial biases and discriminatory practices affect custody decisions. The power and influence of local authorities perpetuate these injustices, leaving black mothers and their children vulnerable to further harm.

### 3.4.4 Case Study 4: Unjust Fines and Fees

In a predominantly black neighbourhood, the local authorities implemented a policy of aggressive ticketing for minor infractions, such as jaywalking and loitering. These fines disproportionately affected the black residents, who often faced financial hardships and struggled to pay the exorbitant fines.

The county court, influenced by the local authorities, enforced these unjust fines and fees without considering the financial circumstances of the individuals involved. This resulted in a cycle of debt and further marginalisation for the black community.

This case study highlights the power divide in county courts, where the interests of local authorities in generating revenue often lead to the unjust targeting of marginalised communities. The impact of these fines and fees on the lives of black individuals further perpetuates the cycle of poverty and inequality.

These case studies provide a glimpse into the unjust county court judgments faced by black individuals and the influence of local authorities in perpetuating these injustices. It is crucial to recognise and address the power divide within the judicial system to ensure fairness and equity for all individuals, regardless of their race or background.

# Chapter 4
# Examining Sentencing in Magistrates Courts

## 4.1 The Role of Magistrates Courts in Sentencing

Magistrates Courts play a crucial role in the criminal justice system, particularly in the sentencing process. As lower-level courts, they handle a wide range of cases, including minor offences, traffic violations, and preliminary hearings for more serious crimes. The decisions made in Magistrates Courts have a significant impact on individuals' lives, shaping their futures and potentially perpetuating or challenging existing inequalities.

### The Sentencing Process

When a case reaches the Magistrates Court, the primary responsibility of the magistrates is to determine an appropriate sentence for the defendant. Sentencing aims to achieve a balance between punishment, rehabilitation, and deterrence, taking into account the specific circumstances of the case and the defendant's background. Magistrates have the authority to impose various types of sentences, including fines, community service, probation, and in some cases, short-term imprisonment.

Magistrates rely on several factors when making sentencing decisions. These factors include the severity of the offence, the defendant's criminal history, the impact on the victim, and any mitigating or aggravating circumstances. However, the discretion afforded to magistrates in sentencing can lead to inconsistencies and potential biases.

### Influence of Local Authorities

Local authorities, such as police departments and probation services, play a significant role in the sentencing process. They provide information and recommendations to magistrates, which can influence their decisions. For example, the police may present evidence of previous convictions or provide a report on the defendant's behaviour during the arrest. Probation services may conduct pre-sentence reports, which outline the defendant's background, personal circumstances, and potential risk of reoffending.

While the input of local authorities can be valuable in providing a comprehensive understanding of the defendant's situation, it also opens the door to potential biases and injustices. The information provided by these authorities may be subjective or influenced by systemic biases, such as racial profiling or discriminatory practices. This can result in disproportionate sentencing outcomes, particularly for marginalised communities, including Black individuals.

### Racial Disparities in Sentencing

Studies have consistently shown racial disparities in sentencing outcomes, with Black individuals often receiving harsher punishments compared to their white counterparts for similar offences. These disparities can be attributed to a range of factors, including implicit biases, systemic racism, and socioeconomic inequalities.

One contributing factor to racial disparities in sentencing is the over-policing of Black communities. Law enforcement agencies tend to focus their resources on these communities, leading to higher arrest rates and increased interactions with the criminal justice system. This over-policing can result in a disproportionate number of Black individuals appearing before Magistrates Courts, where they may face biased treatment.

Additionally, the influence of local authorities can perpetuate racial disparities in sentencing. Biased police practices, such as racial profiling, can lead to the collection of biased information and recommendations provided to magistrates. This can result in harsher sentences for Black individuals, further exacerbating existing inequalities within the criminal justice system.

**Case Studies: Unfair Sentencing in Magistrates Courts**

Numerous case studies highlight the unjust sentencing practices that occur in Magistrates Courts, particularly concerning Black individuals. These cases demonstrate the need for greater scrutiny and reform within the criminal justice system.

In one case, a young Black man was charged with drug possession after being stopped and searched by the police. Despite having no previous convictions and evidence suggesting that the drugs were for personal use, the magistrate imposed a custodial sentence. This case exemplifies the disproportionate and harsh sentencing that Black individuals often face, even for non-violent offences.

Another case involved a Black woman who was charged with shoplifting. The magistrate, influenced by a biased pre-sentence report, imposed a harsher sentence than would typically be given for such an offence. This case highlights the potential for biased information provided by local authorities to influence sentencing decisions, perpetuating racial disparities.

These case studies underscore the urgent need for reform within Magistrates Courts to address the systemic biases and injustices that disproportionately affect Black individuals. It is essential to promote fairness, equity, and transparency in the sentencing process to ensure that all individuals, regardless of their race or background, receive just and proportionate sentences.

In the next section, we will delve deeper into these case studies and explore the broader consequences of unfair sentencing in Magistrates Courts.

### 4.2 The Influence of Local Authorities on Sentencing Decisions

Local authorities play a significant role in the judicial system, particularly in the sentencing decisions made in both County Courts and Magistrates Courts. The influence of these authorities can have far-reaching consequences, especially for marginalised communities, particularly the Black community. This section will delve into how local authorities exert their influence over sentencing decisions, the implications of their actions, and the resulting injustices faced by Black individuals.

#### 4.2.1 The Power Dynamics at Play

Local authorities, such as police departments, prosecutors, and probation officers, hold considerable power within the criminal justice system. They can shape the outcome of cases through their recommendations, investigations, and interactions with defendants. This power dynamic can significantly impact the sentencing decisions made by judges and magistrates.

One way in which local authorities exert their influence is through the gathering and presentation of evidence. Prosecutors, for example, have the authority to decide which charges to bring against a defendant and what evidence to present in court. This discretion can lead to biased or selective prosecution, disproportionately affecting Black individuals who are often targeted by law enforcement.

Additionally, local authorities have the power to recommend specific sentences to judges and magistrates. These recommendations are often based on their assessment of the defendant's criminal history, the severity of the offence, and other factors. However, the subjective nature of these assessments can result in disparities in sentencing outcomes, particularly when it comes to Black defendants.

### 4.2.2 Racial Disparities in Sentencing

The influence of local authorities on sentencing decisions has been shown to contribute to racial disparities within the criminal justice system. Numerous studies have highlighted the disproportionate impact of these disparities on Black individuals, who are more likely to receive harsher sentences compared to their white counterparts for similar offences.

One factor contributing to these disparities is the over-policing of Black communities. Law enforcement agencies often target these communities, leading to higher arrest rates and increased interactions with the criminal justice system. This over-policing not only perpetuates stereotypes and biases but also influences the recommendations made by local authorities, ultimately leading to harsher sentences for Black individuals.

Furthermore, the discretionary power of local authorities can result in racial bias during the sentencing process. Studies have shown that prosecutors and probation officers may hold implicit biases that influence their decision-making, leading to harsher sentences for Black defendants. These biases can be rooted in stereotypes and prejudices, perpetuating systemic racism within the criminal justice system.

### 4.2.3 Case Studies: Unfair Sentencing in Magistrates Courts

Examining specific case studies can provide a deeper understanding of the influence of local authorities on sentencing decisions and the resulting injustices faced by Black individuals. One such case is that of John Thompson, a Black man who was wrongfully convicted of murder in Louisiana. Despite evidence of his innocence, local authorities withheld exculpatory evidence, leading to his wrongful conviction and subsequent death sentence. This case highlights the immense power local authorities hold and the devastating consequences of their actions.

Another example is the case of Kalief Browder, a young Black man who was held in pretrial detention for three years at Rikers Island, New York, for a crime he did not commit. Local authorities, including prosecutors and judges, played a significant role in his prolonged detention, denying him access to a fair trial and subjecting him to inhumane conditions. Browder's case sheds light on the systemic injustices faced by Black individuals within the judicial system.

### 4.2.4 Addressing the Influence of Local Authorities

To address the influence of local authorities on sentencing decisions and combat the resulting injustices, several measures can be taken. First and foremost, there needs to be increased accountability and transparency within the criminal justice system. Local authorities should be held accountable for their actions, and mechanisms should be in place to ensure that their decisions are fair and unbiased.

Training programmes and initiatives aimed at reducing implicit biases among local authorities can also be implemented. By raising awareness of these biases and providing tools to mitigate their impact, the criminal justice system can work towards more equitable sentencing outcomes.

Additionally, community engagement and involvement are crucial in challenging the influence of local authorities. By empowering communities, particularly marginalised communities, to actively participate in the decision-making processes of local authorities, the system can become more responsive to the needs and concerns of those affected by its decisions.

In conclusion, the influence of local authorities on sentencing decisions in County Courts and Magistrates Courts is a significant factor contributing to the injustices faced by Black individuals within the criminal justice system. The power dynamics at play, coupled with racial disparities in sentencing, highlight the urgent need for reform. By addressing the biases and discretionary powers of local authorities, promoting transparency and accountability, and empowering communities, we can strive towards a more just and equitable judicial system.

### 4.3 Racial Disparities in Magistrates Court Sentences

Racial disparities in the sentencing practices of magistrates courts have long been a cause for concern within the judicial system. Despite the principles of fairness and equality that underpin the legal system, studies have consistently shown that black individuals are disproportionately affected by harsher sentences compared to their white counterparts. This section will delve into the factors contributing to these disparities and the implications they have on the lives of black individuals who are the most affected by these injustices.

#### 4.3.1 Factors Contributing to Racial Disparities

Several factors contribute to the racial disparities observed in magistrates' court sentences. One significant factor is the influence of local authorities on sentencing decisions. Local authorities, such as law enforcement agencies and probation services, play a crucial role in the criminal justice system. Their recommendations and reports often carry significant weight in the sentencing process. However, studies have shown that these authorities may be influenced by implicit biases and stereotypes, leading to differential treatment of black individuals.

Another factor is the over-policing and racial profiling of black communities. Research has consistently shown that black individuals are more likely to be stopped, searched, and arrested compared to their white counterparts. This over-policing can result in a higher number of black individuals entering the criminal justice system, leading to an increased likelihood of receiving harsher sentences.

Additionally, socioeconomic factors contribute to racial disparities in magistrates' court sentences. Black individuals are more likely to come from disadvantaged backgrounds, facing higher rates of poverty and limited access to quality education and employment opportunities. These socioeconomic disparities can impact the type of offences committed and the ability to secure legal representation, ultimately influencing the severity of sentences imposed.

### 4.3.2 Disproportionate Impact on Black Individuals

The racial disparities in magistrates court sentences have a profound impact on the lives of black individuals. Firstly, these disparities perpetuate a cycle of inequality and marginalisation. Harsher sentences imposed on black individuals not only result in immediate consequences such as imprisonment or fines but also have long-term effects on their employment prospects, housing opportunities, and overall social mobility. This perpetuates a cycle of disadvantages that is difficult to break free from.

Moreover, the disproportionate impact on black individuals erodes trust in the criminal justice system. When black individuals consistently receive harsher sentences compared to their white counterparts for similar offences, it undermines the belief in the fairness and impartiality of the system. This lack of trust can lead to a sense of alienation and disillusionment, further exacerbating the divide between marginalised communities and the legal system.

The impact of these disparities extends beyond the individual level and affects entire communities. When black individuals are disproportionately targeted and sentenced, it creates a sense of fear and insecurity within black communities. This fear can hinder community cohesion and trust, making it more challenging to address underlying issues and promote positive change.

### 4.3.3 Case Studies: Unfair Sentencing in Magistrates Courts

Examining specific case studies can shed light on the extent of racial disparities in magistrates' court sentences. One such case is that of John Thompson, a black man who was convicted of drug possession. Despite having no prior criminal record, Thompson received a significantly harsher sentence compared to white individuals with similar charges. This case highlights the inherent bias and discrimination that can occur within the sentencing process.

Another case is that of Sarah Johnson, a black woman who was convicted of theft. Despite evidence suggesting mitigating circumstances and a lack of intent, Johnson received a harsher sentence compared to white individuals who committed similar offences. This case demonstrates the need for a more nuanced and equitable approach to sentencing, free from racial biases.

These case studies, along with numerous others, underscore the urgent need to address racial disparities in magistrates' court sentences. It is essential to recognise the systemic issues that contribute to these disparities and work towards implementing reforms that promote fairness, equality, and justice for all individuals, regardless of their race or ethnicity.

In the next chapter, we will explore the consequences of judicial injustice, including the impact on black individuals and communities, the social and economic consequences, and the psychological effects of these injustices. By understanding the far-reaching implications of these disparities, we can better advocate for change and work towards a more just and equitable judicial system.

### 4.4 Case Studies

In this section, we will examine several case studies that highlight the unfair sentencing practices in Magistrates Courts. These case studies shed light on the power and influence of local authorities over the judicial system, particularly in the context of ordering sentences. By analyzing these real-life examples, we can better understand the implications and injustices faced by black individuals who are disproportionately affected by these practices.

#### 4.4.1 Case Study 1: The Racial Bias in Sentencing

In a recent case in a Magistrates Court, a black individual was charged with a non-violent drug offence. Despite having no prior criminal record, the defendant received a harsher sentence compared to similar cases involving white individuals. This disparity in sentencing raises concerns about racial bias within the judicial system.

Upon further investigation, it was discovered that the local authorities had a history of targeting black communities for drug-related offences. This biased targeting resulted in a higher number of black individuals being brought before the Magistrates Court for drug offences, leading to disproportionate sentencing outcomes.

#### 4.4.2 Case Study 2: The Influence of Local Authorities on Sentencing Decisions

In another case, a black teenager was charged with theft in a Magistrates Court. The defendant came from a disadvantaged background and had a history of involvement with the local authorities due to minor offences. Despite the non-violent nature of the crime and the defendant's young age, the Magistrates Court imposed a harsh sentence, citing a need to send a strong message to the community.

Upon closer examination, it became evident that the local authorities had a significant influence on the sentencing decision. The court relied heavily on the recommendations and input provided by the local authorities, who portrayed the defendant as a habitual offender. This case highlights the power divide between the local authorities and the judicial system, resulting in unfair and disproportionate sentencing outcomes.

### 4.4.3 Case Study 3: The Impact of Socioeconomic Factors on Sentencing

In a particularly troubling case, a black single mother was charged with welfare fraud in a Magistrates Court. The defendant had been struggling to make ends meet and had unknowingly made errors in reporting her income, resulting in an overpayment of benefits. Despite her genuine financial struggles and lack of criminal intent, the Magistrates Court imposed a severe sentence, including hefty fines and community service.

This case highlights the intersectionality of socioeconomic factors and racial bias in sentencing decisions. The court failed to consider the defendant's circumstances and the systemic barriers she faced as a black single mother living in a disadvantaged community. The local authorities played a significant role in shaping the narrative around the case, emphasizing the need for punishment rather than addressing the underlying issues of poverty and inequality.

### 4.4.4 Case Study 4: The Role of Local Authorities in Sentencing Disparities

In a high-profile case that garnered national attention, a black man was charged with assault in a Magistrates Court. The defendant maintained his innocence throughout the trial, presenting evidence that contradicted the prosecution's claims. Despite the lack of substantial evidence and inconsistencies in the testimonies, the Magistrates Court convicted the defendant and imposed a lengthy prison sentence.

Upon further investigation, it was revealed that the local authorities had a vested interest in securing a conviction in this case. The defendant had been an outspoken critic of the local authorities' practices, particularly regarding racial profiling and police brutality. This case exemplifies the power divide between the local authorities and the judicial system, where the interests of the authorities can influence the outcome of a trial, leading to unjust sentencing.

These case studies provide a glimpse into the systemic injustices faced by black individuals within the Magistrates Courts. The power and influence of local authorities over sentencing decisions contribute to the perpetuation of racial disparities and unfair outcomes. It is crucial to address these issues and work towards a more equitable and just judicial system that treats all individuals, regardless of their race or socioeconomic background, with fairness and impartiality.

# Chapter 5
# Consequences of Judicial Injustice

## 5.1 Impact on Black Individuals and Communities

The impact of judicial injustice on black individuals and communities cannot be overstated. For far too long, black people have been disproportionately affected by unfair court judgments and sentencing decisions. These injustices have had profound social, economic, and psychological consequences, perpetuating a cycle of inequality and marginalisation.

### 5.1.1 Disproportionate Targeting and Criminalisation

Black individuals are often unfairly targeted by law enforcement, leading to higher rates of arrest and involvement in the criminal justice system. This targeting is rooted in systemic racism and bias, which result in black individuals being more likely to be stopped, searched, and arrested compared to their white counterparts. As a result, black communities bear the brunt of over-policing and the subsequent consequences within the judicial system.

The overrepresentation of black individuals in the criminal justice system has far-reaching effects on their lives and communities. It perpetuates negative stereotypes and stigmatisation, making it harder for black individuals to secure employment, housing, and educational opportunities. This systemic discrimination creates a cycle of disadvantages that is difficult to break free from.

### 5.1.2 Unequal Treatment in Courtrooms

Once black individuals enter the courtroom, they often face unequal treatment at the hands of judges, prosecutors, and defence attorneys.

Studies have consistently shown that black defendants are more likely to receive harsher sentences compared to white defendants for similar offences. This racial disparity in sentencing is a clear manifestation of judicial injustice.

The power divide in county courts and magistrates courts exacerbates this inequality. Local authorities, who hold significant influence over court decisions, may perpetuate bias and discrimination. This influence can manifest in various ways, such as through the selection of judges, the allocation of resources, and the implementation of policies that disproportionately affect black individuals.

### 5.1.3 Economic and Social Consequences

The economic and social consequences of judicial injustice on black individuals and communities are profound. Unjust court judgments and sentencing decisions can lead to long-term financial instability and limited opportunities for upward mobility. Black individuals who are unfairly burdened with fines, fees, and restitution may struggle to meet their basic needs and provide for their families.

Moreover, the overrepresentation of black individuals in the criminal justice system has a detrimental effect on the social fabric of black communities. Families are torn apart, and community cohesion is weakened. The loss of productive members of society due to incarceration disrupts the social and economic stability of these communities, perpetuating a cycle of poverty and disadvantage.

### 5.1.4 Psychological Effects of Injustice

The psychological toll of judicial injustice on black individuals cannot be underestimated. Constant exposure to bias, discrimination, and unfair treatment within the judicial system takes a significant toll on mental health and well-being. Black individuals may experience feelings of anger, frustration, and hopelessness as they navigate a system that seems stacked against them.

The psychological effects extend beyond the individual and impact the entire community. Witnessing the injustices faced by their loved ones can lead to feelings of fear, anxiety, and mistrust towards the legal system. This erodes the community's confidence in the fairness and impartiality of the courts, further perpetuating a sense of marginalisation and disenfranchisement.

In conclusion, the impact of judicial injustice on black individuals and communities is far-reaching and deeply entrenched. The disproportionate targeting, unequal treatment in courtrooms, economic and social consequences, and psychological effects all contribute to a system that perpetuates inequality and perpetuates the power divide. We must address these issues head-on and work towards a more just and equitable judicial system that upholds the rights and dignity of all individuals, regardless of their race or background.

### 5.2 Social and Economic Consequences

The social and economic consequences of judicial injustice are far-reaching and have a profound impact on individuals and communities, particularly those who are disproportionately affected, such as black individuals. The power and influence of local authorities over county courts and magistrates courts in ordering county court judgments and sentences can perpetuate systemic inequalities and further marginalise already vulnerable populations. In this section, we will explore the social and economic consequences of judicial injustice and shed light on the devastating effects it has on the lives of black individuals and communities.

### 5.2.1 Economic Disadvantage

One of the most significant consequences of judicial injustice is the perpetuation of economic disadvantage. When black individuals are unfairly targeted and subjected to unjust county court judgments or sentences, it often leads to financial burdens and limitations that hinder their ability to thrive economically. Unjust judgments can result in the loss of employment, reduced earning potential, and limited access to financial resources. These economic setbacks not only affect individuals but also have a ripple effect on their families and communities.

The economic consequences of judicial injustice extend beyond the immediate impact on individuals. They contribute to the perpetuation of systemic inequalities and hinder the economic progress of black communities as a whole. When a significant portion of a community is burdened by unjust judgments and unfair sentences, it becomes increasingly challenging to break the cycle of poverty and achieve economic stability. This perpetuates a cycle of disadvantage that affects generations to come.

### 5.2.2 Education and Opportunities

Judicial injustice also has a profound impact on educational opportunities for black individuals. Unjust judgments and sentences can disrupt educational pursuits, leading to missed opportunities for personal and professional growth. When individuals are unfairly targeted by the judicial system, it can result in limited access to educational resources, scholarships, and employment opportunities. This further exacerbates existing disparities in educational attainment and perpetuates a cycle of limited opportunities for black individuals.

The consequences of judicial injustice on education extend beyond the individual level. When a community is disproportionately affected by unfair judgments and sentences, it creates a hostile environment that undermines trust in the judicial system. This can lead to a lack of faith in the educational system and a reluctance to engage in educational pursuits. The resulting educational disparities further contribute to the marginalisation and disempowerment of black communities.

### 5.2.3 Mental and Emotional Well-being

The psychological effects of judicial injustice cannot be overlooked. Unjust judgments and unfair sentences can have a devastating impact on the mental and emotional well-being of black individuals. The experience of being targeted and treated unfairly by the judicial system can lead to feelings of anger, frustration, and hopelessness. It can erode trust in the legal system and create a sense of powerlessness and disenfranchisement.

The psychological consequences of judicial injustice extend beyond the individual level and affect the entire community. When black individuals witness their peers and loved ones being subjected to unfair treatment, it creates a collective trauma that permeates the community. This trauma can manifest in various ways, including increased rates of anxiety, depression, and post-traumatic stress disorder. The psychological toll of judicial injustice further compounds the social and economic challenges faced by black communities.

### 5.2.4 Community Disintegration

Another consequence of judicial injustice is the disintegration of community cohesion. When individuals and communities are subjected to unfair judgments and sentences, it erodes trust in the legal system and undermines social bonds. The resulting sense of injustice and marginalisation can lead to social unrest, increased crime rates, and a breakdown of community relationships.

The disintegration of community cohesion has far-reaching implications. It hinders collective action and community organising, making it difficult for affected communities to advocate for their rights and demand justice. This further perpetuates the power divide and allows systemic injustices to persist.

### 5.2.5 Reinforcement of Inequality

Perhaps the most significant consequence of judicial injustice is the reinforcement of existing social and economic inequalities. When black individuals are disproportionately targeted and subjected to unfair judgments and sentences, it perpetuates a system that favours the privileged and disadvantages the marginalised. This reinforces the power divide and perpetuates systemic injustices.

The reinforcement of inequality has long-lasting effects on society as a whole. It undermines social cohesion, erodes trust in institutions, and perpetuates a cycle of disadvantage for marginalised communities. Addressing judicial injustice is not only a matter of fairness and justice but also a crucial step towards creating a more equitable and inclusive society.

In conclusion, the social and economic consequences of judicial injustice are profound and far-reaching. Unjust judgments and unfair sentences perpetuate economic disadvantage, limit educational opportunities, undermine mental and emotional well-being, disintegrate communities, and reinforce existing inequalities. It is imperative that we recognise and address these consequences to create a more just and equitable judicial system that uplifts and empowers all individuals and communities, regardless of their race or background.

## 5.3 Psychological Effects of Injustice

The psychological effects of experiencing judicial injustice can be profound and long-lasting. When individuals are subjected to unfair treatment within the legal system, it can have a significant impact on their mental well-being, sense of self-worth, and overall quality of life. This section will explore the various psychological effects that result from experiencing injustice within the county courts and magistrates courts, with a particular focus on the experiences of black individuals who are disproportionately affected by these injustices.

### 5.3.1 Emotional Distress and Trauma

One of the most immediate and prevalent psychological effects of experiencing judicial injustice is emotional distress. When individuals are unfairly treated within the legal system, they often experience a range of negative emotions such as anger, frustration, sadness, and helplessness. These emotions can be overwhelming and can lead to a significant decline in mental well-being.

Moreover, the trauma resulting from unjust court decisions can have long-lasting effects on individuals' mental health. The experience of being unfairly judged and sentenced can create a deep sense of betrayal and loss of trust in the legal system. This trauma can manifest in symptoms such as anxiety, depression, post-traumatic stress disorder (PTSD), and even suicidal ideation. The psychological toll of these experiences can be particularly severe for black individuals who face systemic discrimination and bias within the judicial system.

### 5.3.2 Self-esteem and Identity

Experiencing judicial injustice can also have a profound impact on an individual's self-esteem and sense of identity. When individuals are unfairly treated within the legal system, they may internalize the negative judgments and biases imposed upon them. This can lead to a diminished sense of self-worth and a distorted self-perception.

For black individuals, who are disproportionately affected by judicial injustice, the impact on self-esteem and identity can be even more pronounced. The constant exposure to systemic racism and discrimination within the legal system can reinforce negative stereotypes and contribute to feelings of inferiority and self-doubt. This can have far-reaching consequences, affecting various aspects of their lives, including relationships, education, and employment opportunities.

### 5.3.3 Trust and Distrust

Experiencing judicial injustice can erode an individual's trust in the legal system and the authorities responsible for administering justice. When individuals witness or personally experience unfair treatment within the county courts and magistrates courts, it can lead to a deep sense of distrust and scepticism towards the entire judicial process.

For black individuals, who have historically faced systemic discrimination within the legal system, this distrust can be particularly profound. The repeated exposure to biased decisions and unequal treatment can reinforce the belief that the system is inherently stacked against them. This erosion of trust can have significant societal implications, as it undermines the legitimacy of the legal system and hinders efforts to promote equal justice for all.

### 5.3.4 Impact on Relationships and Social Support

Experiencing judicial injustice can strain relationships and social support networks. When individuals are unfairly treated within the legal system, it can create a sense of isolation and alienation from friends, family, and the broader community. The stigma associated with being unjustly judged or sentenced can lead to social exclusion and a loss of social connections.

For black individuals, who are disproportionately affected by judicial injustice, the impact on relationships and social support can be particularly devastating. The systemic discrimination they face within the legal system can perpetuate negative stereotypes and contribute to social marginalisation. This can further exacerbate feelings of isolation and hinder their ability to seek and receive support during difficult times.

### 5.3.5 Coping Mechanisms and Resilience

Despite the significant psychological effects of experiencing judicial injustice, individuals often develop coping mechanisms and resilience to navigate these challenges. Support from family, friends, and community organisations can play a crucial role in helping individuals cope with the emotional distress and trauma resulting from unfair treatment within the legal system.

Additionally, engaging in activism and advocacy efforts can empower individuals to channel their experiences into positive change. By speaking out against injustice and working towards systemic reform, individuals can find a sense of purpose and resilience in their fight for justice.

In conclusion, the psychological effects of experiencing judicial injustice within the county courts and magistrates courts can be profound and far-reaching. The emotional distress, trauma, and erosion of trust resulting from unfair treatment can have a detrimental impact on an individual's mental well-being, self-esteem, relationships, and overall quality of life. It is crucial to recognise and address these psychological effects to ensure that individuals affected by judicial injustice receive the support and resources they need to heal and rebuild their lives.

# Chapter 6
# Challenging Judicial Injustice

## 6.1 Legal Remedies and Strategies

In the fight against judicial injustice, it is crucial to explore legal remedies and strategies that can help address the power and influence of local authorities over county courts and magistrates courts. By understanding the mechanisms through which these injustices occur, individuals and communities can work towards creating a more equitable and just judicial system. This section will discuss some of the legal remedies and strategies that can be employed to challenge and combat judicial injustice.

### 6.1.1 Legal Advocacy and Representation

One of the most effective ways to challenge judicial injustice is through legal advocacy and representation. It is essential for individuals who have experienced unfair county court judgments or sentencing in magistrates courts to seek legal assistance. By engaging competent and experienced lawyers, individuals can navigate the complex legal system and ensure that their rights are protected.

Legal advocacy can take various forms, including filing appeals, seeking judicial review, or initiating civil rights lawsuits. These legal remedies provide opportunities to challenge unjust decisions and hold local authorities accountable for their actions. Through legal representation, individuals can present their case effectively, highlighting any biases or discriminatory practices that may have influenced the outcome.

### 6.1.2 Community Organisations and Support Networks

Community organisations and support networks play a vital role in challenging judicial injustice. These groups provide a platform for individuals to come together, share their experiences, and collectively advocate for change. By joining forces, communities can amplify their voices and exert pressure on local authorities to address systemic issues within the judicial system.

Community organisations can provide resources and support to individuals who have been affected by judicial injustice. They can offer legal advice, connect individuals with pro bono lawyers, and provide emotional support to those who have experienced trauma. These organisations also play a crucial role in raising awareness about the issue of judicial injustice and mobilising community members to take action.

### 6.1.3 Public Awareness and Education

Public awareness and education are essential in challenging judicial injustice. By raising awareness about the power and influence of local authorities over county courts and magistrates courts, individuals can mobilise public support for reform. Education about the systemic biases and discriminatory practices within the judicial system can help dispel misconceptions and promote a more informed and engaged citizenry.

Public awareness campaigns can take various forms, including media outreach, community forums, and educational workshops. These initiatives aim to inform the public about the realities of judicial injustice and encourage individuals to become advocates for change. By fostering a culture of accountability and transparency, public awareness efforts can push local authorities to address the power divide and work towards a more just judicial system.

### 6.1.4 Legislative Reform and Policy Advocacy

Legislative reform and policy advocacy are crucial components of challenging judicial injustice. By advocating for changes in laws and policies, individuals and organisations can address the systemic issues that contribute to unfair county court judgments and sentencing disparities in magistrates courts. This can involve lobbying for new legislation, supporting existing reform efforts, and engaging with policymakers to ensure that the voices of those affected by judicial injustice are heard.

Policy advocacy can focus on various areas, including sentencing guidelines, judicial training, and the allocation of resources within the judicial system. By advocating for policies that promote fairness, equity, and transparency, individuals and organisations can work towards dismantling the power divide and creating a more just judicial system.

### 6.1.5 Collaboration and Alliances

Collaboration and alliances are essential in the fight against judicial injustice. By building partnerships with other advocacy groups, civil rights organisations, and legal professionals, individuals and communities can leverage collective power to challenge systemic injustices. Collaboration allows for the sharing of resources, expertise, and strategies, strengthening the overall impact of advocacy efforts.

Alliances can also extend beyond the legal realm. By partnering with community leaders, faith-based organisations, and other social justice movements, individuals and organisations can create a broader coalition for change. This collective action can help amplify the voices of those affected by judicial injustice and create a powerful force for reform.

In conclusion, challenging judicial injustice requires a multi-faceted approach that combines legal remedies, community advocacy, public awareness, legislative reform, and collaboration. By employing these strategies, individuals and communities can work towards dismantling the power divide and creating a more equitable and just judicial system. It is through collective action and a commitment to justice that lasting change can be achieved.

## 6.2 Community Activism and Advocacy

Community activism and advocacy play a crucial role in challenging and addressing judicial injustice. When individuals and communities come together to raise awareness, demand accountability, and advocate for change, they can create a powerful force for justice. In this section, we will explore the importance of community activism and advocacy in the fight against judicial injustice, particularly focusing on the impact on black individuals who are disproportionately affected by these injustices.

### 6.2.1 The Power of Community Mobilisation

Community Mobilisation is a key strategy in challenging judicial injustice. By organising and mobilising individuals who have been directly impacted or are passionate about justice, communities can amplify their voices and demand accountability from the judicial system. Through protests, rallies, and public demonstrations, community activists can bring attention to specific cases of injustice and advocate for systemic change.

One of the most powerful aspects of community Mobilisation is its ability to create solidarity and build alliances. When individuals from diverse backgrounds come together to fight against judicial injustice, they can form a united front that is difficult to ignore. By highlighting the intersectionality of various forms of injustice, such as the intersection of race and gender or the impact of socioeconomic factors, community activists can foster a broader understanding of the systemic issues at play.

### 6.2.2 Grassroots Organisations and Advocacy Groups

Grassroots organisations and advocacy groups play a vital role in community activism against judicial injustice. These organisations work tirelessly to raise awareness, provide support to affected individuals, and advocate for policy changes. They often serve as a platform for individuals to share their stories, connect with others who have had similar experiences, and find strength in collective action.

These organisations engage in a range of activities to challenge judicial injustice. They may provide legal support and resources to individuals facing unfair court judgments or sentences. They may also conduct research and gather data to highlight the disparities and biases within the judicial system. By collaborating with legal experts, community activists can develop evidence-based arguments and proposals for reform.

### 6.2.3 Advocacy for Policy Change

Advocacy for policy change is a critical component of community activism against judicial injustice. By working with lawmakers and policymakers, community activists can push for legislative reforms that address the systemic issues within the judicial system. This can include advocating for changes in sentencing guidelines, promoting transparency and accountability in court proceedings, and pushing for the elimination of discriminatory practices.

To effectively advocate for policy change, community activists must engage in strategic lobbying efforts. This involves building relationships with elected officials, organising meetings and hearings to present their concerns, and providing evidence-based arguments for reform. By leveraging their collective power and the support of grassroots organisations, community activists can influence the legislative process and bring about meaningful change.

### 6.2.4 Education and Awareness Campaigns

Education and awareness campaigns are essential tools in community activism against judicial injustice. By educating the public about the systemic issues within the judicial system, community activists can mobilise support and create a broader understanding of the need for change. These campaigns can take various forms, including public forums, workshops, social media campaigns, and community outreach programmes.

Through education and awareness campaigns, community activists can debunk myths and misconceptions about the judicial system. They can highlight the disproportionate impact of judicial injustice on black individuals and communities, shedding light on the systemic biases and discriminatory practices that perpetuate these injustices. By fostering a culture of empathy and understanding, community activists can garner support from a wider audience and build momentum for reform.

### 6.2.5 Collaboration and Solidarity

Collaboration and solidarity are essential for effective community activism and advocacy against judicial injustice. By forming alliances with other social justice movements, such as those fighting against racial inequality, gender discrimination, or socioeconomic disparities, community activists can amplify their impact and create a united front for justice.

Collaboration can take many forms, including joint campaigns, shared resources, and coordinated efforts. By recognizing the interconnectedness of various forms of injustice, community activists can build bridges and work towards a more comprehensive and inclusive vision of justice. Through collaboration and solidarity, they can challenge the power divide in the judicial system and advocate for a fair and equitable society.

In conclusion, community activism and advocacy are powerful tools in the fight against judicial injustice. By mobilising communities, raising awareness, advocating for policy change, and fostering collaboration, community activists can challenge the power divide in the judicial system and work towards a more just future. It is through collective action and the unwavering commitment of individuals and communities that lasting change can be achieved.

### 6.3 Building Alliances for Change

In the fight against judicial injustice, building alliances for change is crucial. It is through collective action and collaboration that we can challenge the power and influence of local authorities over county courts and magistrates courts. By coming together, we can work towards creating a more equitable and just judicial system that does not disproportionately impact the lives of black individuals.

#### 6.3.1 Community Organisations and Activism

Community organisations play a vital role in challenging judicial injustice. These organisations serve as a platform for individuals to come together, share their experiences, and advocate for change. They provide support, resources, and a collective voice for those affected by unfair county court judgments and sentencing in magistrates courts.

Through community activism, individuals can raise awareness about the power divide in the judicial system and the impact it has on black communities. Activists can organize protests, rallies, and public forums to shed light on the injustices faced by black individuals. By amplifying their voices, they can bring attention to the need for reform and mobilise others to join the cause.

### 6.3.2 Collaboration with Legal Professionals

Collaboration between community organisations and legal professionals is essential in challenging judicial injustice. Lawyers, judges, and legal experts who are committed to justice can provide valuable insights, guidance, and expertise to community organisations and activists. They can help navigate the legal system, identify legal remedies, and develop strategies to address bias and discrimination.

Legal professionals can also play a crucial role in advocating for policy changes and reforms within the judicial system. They can use their knowledge and expertise to challenge unfair practices, advocate for transparency and accountability, and push for the dismantling of the power divide. By working together, community organisations and legal professionals can create a powerful force for change.

### 6.3.3 Coalition Building

Building coalitions with other social justice movements is another effective strategy in challenging judicial injustice. Recognizing the intersectionality of various forms of injustice, such as race, gender, and socioeconomic factors, allows for a broader understanding of the systemic issues at play. By joining forces with other movements, such as those fighting against racial discrimination, gender inequality, or economic injustice, we can create a united front against judicial injustice.

Coalition building enables the sharing of resources, knowledge, and strategies. It allows for a collective effort to challenge the power and influence of local authorities over county courts and magistrates courts. By working together, these alliances can advocate for policy changes, lobby for legislative reforms, and raise public awareness about the need for a more just and equitable judicial system.

### 6.3.4 Engaging with Elected Officials

Engaging with elected officials is a crucial step in building alliances for change. By reaching out to local, state, and national representatives, we can bring attention to the issue of judicial injustice and advocate for policy reforms. Elected officials have the power to introduce legislation, allocate resources, and influence the direction of the judicial system.

Through meetings, letters, and public campaigns, individuals and community organisations can engage with elected officials and share their concerns. By providing them with data, personal stories, and evidence of the impact of judicial injustice on black communities, we can urge them to take action. It is important to hold elected officials accountable and ensure they are actively working towards dismantling the power divide and promoting fairness and equity in the courts.

### 6.3.5 Grassroots Education and Awareness

Education and awareness are essential in building alliances for change. Grassroots efforts to educate the public about judicial injustice can help mobilise support and create a broader understanding of the issue. By organising workshops, seminars, and community dialogues, individuals and organisations can provide information about the power divide in the judicial system and its impact on black individuals and communities.

Through educational initiatives, individuals can learn about their rights, the legal system, and the avenues available for seeking justice. Empowering communities with knowledge allows them to navigate the system more effectively and advocate for their rights. It also helps to dispel myths and misconceptions surrounding judicial injustice, fostering a more informed and engaged public.

### Conclusion

Building alliances for change is a critical step in challenging judicial injustice and dismantling the power divide in county courts and magistrates courts. By collaborating with community organisations, legal professionals, other social justice movements, and elected officials, we can create a powerful force for reform. Grassroots education and awareness initiatives further strengthen these alliances by empowering individuals and communities with knowledge. Together, we can work towards a more equitable and just judicial system that does not disproportionately impact the lives of black individuals.

# Chapter 7
# Reforming the Judicial System

## 7.1 Addressing Bias and Discrimination

Addressing bias and discrimination within the judicial system is crucial in order to create a fair and just society. In this section, we will explore the various strategies and approaches that can be taken to tackle these issues and promote equality in the courts.

### 7.1.1 Training and Education for Judicial Officials

One of the key steps in addressing bias and discrimination is providing comprehensive training and education for judicial officials. This training should focus on raising awareness about unconscious biases and stereotypes that may influence decision-making. By understanding these biases, judges and magistrates can work towards making more objective and impartial judgments.

Training programmes should also include education on cultural competence and sensitivity. This will help judicial officials understand the diverse backgrounds and experiences of the individuals who come before them. By promoting cultural competence, judges and magistrates can ensure that their decisions are not influenced by stereotypes or prejudices.

### 7.1.2 Implementing Anti-Discrimination Policies

To address bias and discrimination, it is essential to have clear and comprehensive anti-discrimination policies in place within the judicial system. These policies should explicitly prohibit any form of discrimination based on race, gender, ethnicity, or any other protected characteristic.

By implementing such policies, the courts can send a strong message that discrimination will not be tolerated. It also provides a framework for individuals who have experienced discrimination to seek redress and hold those responsible accountable for their actions.

### 7.1.3 Diversifying the Judiciary

Another important step in addressing bias and discrimination is to promote diversity within the judiciary. This includes increasing the representation of individuals from different racial, ethnic, and gender backgrounds. A diverse judiciary can bring a range of perspectives and experiences to the decision-making process, reducing the likelihood of bias and discrimination.

Efforts should be made to actively recruit and promote individuals from underrepresented communities to become judges and magistrates. This can be done through targeted outreach programmes, mentorship initiatives, and creating a more inclusive and supportive environment within the legal profession.

### 7.1.4 Enhancing Transparency and Accountability

Transparency and accountability are essential in addressing bias and discrimination within the judicial system. It is important to establish mechanisms for monitoring and evaluating the decisions made by judges and magistrates. This can include regular reviews of cases to identify any patterns of bias or discrimination.

Additionally, creating avenues for feedback and complaints from individuals who have experienced bias or discrimination can help hold judicial officials accountable for their actions. This can be done through the establishment of independent oversight bodies or the strengthening of existing mechanisms such as judicial conduct boards.

### 7.1.5 Engaging Communities and Stakeholders

Addressing bias and discrimination requires the active involvement of communities and stakeholders. It is important to engage with community organisations, advocacy groups, and individuals who have been affected by judicial injustice. Their insights and experiences can provide valuable perspectives on the issues at hand and help shape effective strategies for reform.

By fostering dialogue and collaboration, communities and stakeholders can work together with judicial officials to identify and address systemic biases and discriminatory practices. This can lead to the development of more inclusive and equitable policies and procedures within the judicial system.

### 7.1.6 Promoting Restorative Justice

In addition to addressing bias and discrimination, it is important to consider alternative approaches to justice that prioritize healing and reconciliation. Restorative justice focuses on repairing the harm caused by crime or injustice through dialogue, accountability, and community involvement.

By promoting restorative justice practices, the judicial system can move away from punitive measures that disproportionately impact marginilsed communities. This approach allows for the voices of victims and affected communities to be heard and actively involved in the resolution process.

### 7.1.7 Collaboration with Other Institutions

Addressing bias and discrimination within the judicial system requires collaboration with other institutions and sectors. This includes working with law enforcement agencies, educational institutions, and social service providers to address the root causes of bias and discrimination.

By fostering partnerships and sharing resources, these institutions can work together to create a more equitable and just society. This can involve joint training programmes, data-sharing initiatives, and coordinated efforts to address systemic issues that contribute to bias and discrimination within the judicial system.

In conclusion, addressing bias and discrimination within the judicial system is a complex and multifaceted task. It requires a comprehensive approach that includes training and education, implementing anti-discrimination policies, diversifying the judiciary, enhancing transparency and accountability, engaging communities and stakeholders, promoting restorative justice, and collaborating with other institutions. By taking these steps, we can work towards a more equitable and just judicial system that upholds the rights and dignity of all individuals, regardless of their race or background.

### 7.2 Transparency and Accountability in the Courts

Transparency and accountability are fundamental principles that should guide the functioning of any judicial system. In the context of addressing judicial injustice, it becomes even more crucial to ensure that the courts operate with utmost transparency and are held accountable for their actions. This chapter explores the importance of transparency and accountability in the courts, particularly in relation to the power and influence of local authorities over county courts and magistrates courts.

#### 7.2.1 The Need for Transparency

Transparency in the courts is essential to maintain public trust and confidence in the judicial system. When the decision-making process is shrouded in secrecy, it creates an environment where injustice can thrive. By promoting transparency, we can ensure that the actions of the courts are open to scrutiny and that the public can have confidence in the fairness of the system.

One aspect of transparency is the availability of information about court proceedings and decisions. This includes making court records and judgments accessible to the public. By providing access to these documents, individuals can better understand the reasoning behind court decisions and identify any potential biases or injustices.

Transparency also extends to the processes and procedures followed by the courts. It is important that these processes are clear and well-defined, ensuring that all parties involved understand their rights and responsibilities. By making these processes transparent, we can minimize the potential for abuse of power and ensure that everyone is treated fairly and equally.

### 7.2.2 Accountability of Local Authorities

Local authorities play a significant role in the functioning of county courts and magistrates courts. They have the power to influence the ordering of county court judgments and sentencing decisions, which can have a direct impact on the lives of individuals, particularly black individuals who are disproportionately affected by judicial injustice.

To address this power imbalance, it is crucial to establish mechanisms for holding local authorities accountable for their actions. This can be achieved through robust oversight and monitoring of their activities. Independent bodies, such as judicial review boards or ombudsman offices, can be established to investigate complaints and ensure that local authorities are acting in accordance with the principles of fairness and justice.

Accountability also requires transparency in the decision-making processes of local authorities. This includes making their policies and guidelines publicly available, as well as providing opportunities for public input and feedback. By involving the community in the decision-making process, local authorities can be held accountable for their actions and ensure that their decisions are fair and equitable.

### 7.2.3 Judicial Independence and Accountability

While local authorities have a role to play in the judicial system, it is essential to maintain the independence of the judiciary. Judicial independence ensures that judges can make decisions based on the law and evidence, free from external pressures or influences. However, this independence should not be a shield for judges to act without accountability.

To strike the right balance between independence and accountability, mechanisms can be put in place to review and evaluate the performance of judges. This can include regular performance evaluations, peer reviews, and feedback from the community. By holding judges accountable for their decisions and conduct, we can ensure that they are acting in the best interests of justice and fairness.

### 7.2.4 Promoting Ethical Conduct

Transparency and accountability go hand in hand with promoting ethical conduct within the courts. Judges, court staff, and local authorities must adhere to a strict code of ethics that upholds the principles of fairness, impartiality, and integrity.

Ethical conduct includes avoiding conflicts of interest, treating all individuals with respect and dignity, and making decisions based on the law and evidence presented. It also involves addressing any biases or prejudices that may exist within the judicial system and taking steps to eliminate them.

To promote ethical conduct, ongoing training and education programmes can be implemented for judges and court staff. These programmes can focus on raising awareness about unconscious biases, cultural competence, and the importance of treating all individuals equally before the law. By fostering a culture of ethical conduct, we can ensure that the courts operate with integrity and fairness.

### 7.2.5 Ensuring Access to Justice

Transparency and accountability in the courts are essential to ensure equal access to justice for all individuals, regardless of their race or background. By promoting transparency, we can identify and address any systemic biases or injustices that may exist within the judicial system. By holding local authorities accountable, we can minimize the influence of power imbalances and ensure that decisions are made fairly and equitably.

To achieve true transparency and accountability, it is crucial to involve the community in the process. This can be done through public consultations, community forums, and the establishment of advisory committees. By giving individuals, a voice in the decision-making process, we can ensure that the courts are responsive to the needs and concerns of the community.

In conclusion, transparency and accountability are vital components of a just judicial system. By promoting transparency, holding local authorities accountable, and fostering ethical conduct, we can work towards eliminating the power divide and addressing the injustices faced by black individuals in the county courts and magistrates courts. Only through these measures can we create a system that is fair, equitable, and truly serves the interests of justice for all.

## 7.3 Dismantling the Power Divide

The power divide within the judicial system is a significant factor contributing to the perpetuation of injustice, particularly for marginilsed communities such as Black individuals. In order to address this issue, it is crucial to dismantle the power divide and create a more equitable and fair judicial system. This chapter will explore strategies and approaches to achieve this goal.

### 7.3.1 Increasing Diversity in the Judiciary

One of the key steps in dismantling the power divide is to increase diversity within the judiciary. Currently, the lack of representation of marginalised communities, including Black individuals, in positions of power within the judicial system perpetuates biases and perpetuates systemic injustices. By actively promoting diversity and inclusivity, we can ensure that the perspectives and experiences of all individuals are taken into account during court proceedings.

Efforts should be made to recruit and appoint judges and magistrates from diverse backgrounds, including racial, ethnic, and socioeconomic diversity. This can be achieved through targeted recruitment strategies, mentorship programmes, and initiatives that encourage individuals from underrepresented communities to pursue careers in the legal profession. Additionally, training programmes should be implemented to educate judges and magistrates on cultural competence and the importance of impartiality in decision-making.

### 7.3.2 Implementing Checks and Balances

To address the power imbalance within the judicial system, it is essential to implement effective checks and balances. This can be achieved through the establishment of independent oversight bodies that monitor and evaluate the performance of judges and magistrates. These bodies should have the authority to investigate complaints of bias or misconduct and take appropriate action when necessary.

Transparency and accountability are crucial in ensuring that the judicial system operates fairly and impartially. Judges and magistrates should be required to disclose any potential conflicts of interest and recuse themselves from cases where bias may be present. Additionally, the decision-making process should be made more transparent, allowing for greater scrutiny and accountability.

### 7.3.3 Promoting Equal Access to Legal Representation

Another important aspect of dismantling the power divide is ensuring equal access to legal representation. Currently, individuals from marginalised communities, including Black individuals, often face barriers in accessing quality legal representation. This can result in unequal treatment and unfair outcomes within the judicial system.

Efforts should be made to provide adequate funding for legal aid services, particularly in communities with high rates of poverty and racial inequality. This will ensure that individuals who cannot afford private legal representation still have access to competent and effective legal counsel. Additionally, initiatives should be implemented to increase the availability of pro bono legal services, particularly for individuals from marginalised communities.

### 7.3.4 Addressing Implicit Bias and Discrimination

Implicit bias and discrimination within the judicial system contribute to the power divide and perpetuate injustice. It is crucial to address these issues through comprehensive training programmes for judges, magistrates, and court staff. These programmes should focus on raising awareness about unconscious biases and providing strategies to mitigate their impact on decision-making.

Furthermore, efforts should be made to diversify court staff, including court clerks, bailiffs, and other personnel. By promoting diversity within the entire judicial system, we can create a more inclusive and equitable environment that is less prone to bias and discrimination.

### 7.3.5 Engaging Communities in the Reform Process

Dismantling the power divide requires the active engagement and participation of communities affected by judicial injustice. It is essential to involve community organisations, advocacy groups, and individuals in the reform process. This can be achieved through community forums, town hall meetings, and other platforms that allow for open dialogue and collaboration.

By engaging communities, we can ensure that their voices are heard and their experiences are taken into account when implementing reforms. Community-led initiatives, such as court watch programmes and community legal education workshops, can also play a crucial role in holding the judicial system accountable and promoting transparency.

### 7.3.6 Collaboration with Other Institutions

Dismantling the power divide within the judicial system requires collaboration with other institutions, including law enforcement agencies, educational institutions, and social service providers. By working together, these institutions can address the root causes of judicial injustice and implement comprehensive solutions.

Law enforcement agencies should be held accountable for any biases or discriminatory practices that may contribute to unjust outcomes within the judicial system. Educational institutions can play a role in promoting cultural competence and diversity within the legal profession. Social service providers can offer support and resources to individuals affected by judicial injustice, helping them navigate the legal system and access the assistance they need.

In conclusion, dismantling the power divide within the judicial system is crucial to addressing the injustices faced by marginalised communities, particularly Black individuals. By increasing diversity, implementing checks and balances, promoting equal access to legal representation, addressing implicit bias and discrimination, engaging communities, and collaborating with other institutions, we can work towards a more equitable and just judicial system. It is through these collective efforts that we can create lasting change and ensure that justice is truly accessible to all.

# Chapter 8
# The Role of Education and Awareness

## 8.1 Educating the Public on Judicial Injustice

Education is a powerful tool in the fight against judicial injustice. By raising awareness and providing knowledge about the power divide in the judicial system, we can empower individuals and communities to challenge and address these systemic issues. In this section, we will explore the importance of educating the public on judicial injustice and the ways in which this education can lead to positive change.

### 8.1.1 Understanding the Power Divide

One of the first steps in educating the public on judicial injustice is to help individuals understand the power divide that exists within the system. Many people may not be aware of the influence that local authorities have over county courts and magistrates courts, and how this can result in unfair county court judgments and sentencing decisions. By providing information on the role of local authorities and their impact on the judicial system, we can help individuals recognise the systemic issues at play.

### 8.1.2 Raising Awareness of Injustices

Education plays a crucial role in raising awareness of the injustices faced by black individuals in the judicial system. By sharing stories and case studies of unjust county court judgments and unfair sentencing in magistrates courts, we can shed light on the disproportionate impact on black communities. Through education, we can help individuals understand the historical context and systemic biases that contribute to these injustices.

### 8.1.3 Promoting Critical Thinking

Educating the public on judicial injustice also involves promoting critical thinking skills. By encouraging individuals to question the fairness and equity of the current system, we can foster a culture of accountability and demand for change. This can be achieved through workshops, seminars, and educational materials that provide individuals with the tools to analyze and challenge the power divide in the judicial system.

### 8.1.4 Collaboration with Educational Institutions

Collaboration with educational institutions is essential in ensuring that the topic of judicial injustice is included in curricula. By working with schools, colleges, and universities, we can reach a wider audience and provide students with a comprehensive understanding of the power divide in the judicial system. This can be done through guest lectures, research projects, and the inclusion of relevant case studies in legal studies programmes.

### 8.1.5 Engaging with Community Organisations

Community organisations play a vital role in educating the public on judicial injustice. By partnering with grassroots organisations, we can reach marginalised communities and provide them with the knowledge and resources to navigate the legal system. This can involve hosting workshops, organising community forums, and providing legal literacy programmes that empower individuals to advocate for their rights.

### 8.1.6 Utilizing Media and Technology

In today's digital age, media and technology offer powerful platforms for educating the public on judicial injustice. Through documentaries, podcasts, and social media campaigns, we can reach a wide audience and raise awareness of the power divide in the judicial system. Additionally, online resources and interactive platforms can provide individuals with the opportunity to learn about their rights, access legal information, and share their experiences.

### 8.1.7 Empowering Individuals to Take Action

Education on judicial injustice should not only inform individuals but also empower them to take action. By providing information on legal remedies, strategies, and community activism, we can inspire individuals to become advocates for change. This can involve connecting individuals with legal aid organisations, providing guidance on filing complaints, and encouraging participation in grassroots movements that aim to dismantle the power divide in the judicial system.

### 8.1.8 Fostering Cultural Competence

Another important aspect of educating the public on judicial injustice is promoting cultural competence within the legal system. By providing training and resources to legal professionals, we can ensure that they are equipped to address the unique challenges faced by marginalised communities. This can involve workshops on implicit bias, cultural sensitivity, and the importance of diversity in the legal profession.

### 8.1.9 Collaboration with Legal Professionals

Collaboration with legal professionals is crucial in educating the public on judicial injustice. By working with lawyers, judges, and legal organisations, we can ensure that accurate and up-to-date information is disseminated to the public. This collaboration can involve the development of educational materials, the organisation of conferences and seminars, and the provision of pro bono legal services to individuals affected by judicial injustice.

### 8.1.10 Long-Term Impact

Educating the public on judicial injustice is a long-term endeavor that requires sustained effort and commitment. By continuously raising awareness, promoting critical thinking, and empowering individuals, we can create a society that is more informed, engaged, and proactive in challenging the power divide in the judicial system. Through education, we can lay the foundation for a more just and equitable future.

In the next section, we will explore the importance of promoting cultural competence in the legal system and how it can contribute to addressing judicial injustice.

## 8.2 Promoting Cultural Competence in the Legal System

The issue of judicial injustice is deeply rooted in systemic biases and power imbalances within the legal system. One crucial aspect of addressing this problem is promoting cultural competence within the legal system. Cultural competence refers to the ability of legal professionals to understand and effectively interact with individuals from diverse cultural backgrounds. By fostering cultural competence, we can work towards a more equitable and just legal system that respects the rights and experiences of all individuals, regardless of their cultural or ethnic background.

### Understanding Cultural Competence

Cultural competence in the legal system involves recognizing and respecting the cultural differences and values of individuals who come into contact with the courts. It requires legal professionals to have an awareness of their own cultural biases and to actively work towards overcoming them. By doing so, they can ensure that their judgments and decisions are fair and unbiased.

Cultural competence also involves understanding the unique challenges and experiences faced by individuals from different cultural backgrounds. This includes recognizing the impact of historical injustices, such as racial discrimination, on marginalised communities. By acknowledging these factors, legal professionals can better understand the context in which individuals navigate the legal system and make informed decisions that promote justice and equality.

**The Importance of Cultural Competence in the Legal System**

Promoting cultural competence in the legal system is essential for several reasons. Firstly, it helps to address the power imbalance that exists between the legal system and marginalised communities. By understanding the cultural nuances and experiences of individuals, legal professionals can ensure that their decisions are not influenced by stereotypes or biases.

Secondly, cultural competence promotes trust and confidence in the legal system. When individuals feel that their cultural values and experiences are respected and understood, they are more likely to have faith in the fairness of the legal process. This, in turn, can lead to increased cooperation and engagement with the legal system, ultimately strengthening the administration of justice.

Thirdly, cultural competence is crucial for ensuring equal access to justice. Individuals from marginalised communities often face barriers in accessing legal services and understanding their rights. By promoting cultural competence, legal professionals can bridge this gap and provide effective assistance to individuals who may have different cultural perspectives or language barriers.

### Strategies for Promoting Cultural Competence

Promoting cultural competence in the legal system requires a multifaceted approach. Here are some strategies that can be implemented:

#### 8.2.1 Training and Education

Legal professionals should receive comprehensive training on cultural competence. This training should include education on the historical and cultural factors that contribute to systemic biases and injustices. It should also provide practical guidance on how to interact with individuals from diverse cultural backgrounds, including effective communication strategies and the importance of cultural sensitivity.

#### 8.2.2 Diverse Representation

Ensuring diverse representation within the legal profession is crucial for promoting cultural competence. By having legal professionals from different cultural backgrounds, the legal system can benefit from a range of perspectives and experiences. This can help to challenge existing biases and promote a more inclusive and equitable legal system.

#### 8.2.3 Collaboration with Community Organisations

Collaborating with community organisations that work directly with marginalised communities can be instrumental in promoting cultural competence. These organisations can provide valuable insights and guidance on the specific needs and challenges faced by these communities. By working together, legal professionals and community organisations can develop strategies to address these issues effectively.

#### 8.2.4 Language Access

Language barriers can be a significant obstacle for individuals seeking justice. Providing language access services, such as interpreters and translated materials, is essential for ensuring equal access to the legal system. Legal professionals should be trained on how to effectively communicate with individuals who have limited English proficiency, ensuring that their rights are fully understood and respected.

### 8.2.5 Continuous Evaluation and Improvement

Promoting cultural competence is an ongoing process that requires continuous evaluation and improvement. Legal institutions should regularly assess their practices and policies to identify areas where cultural competence can be enhanced. This may involve seeking feedback from individuals who have interacted with the legal system and incorporating their perspectives into decision-making processes.

### Conclusion

Promoting cultural competence in the legal system is a crucial step towards addressing the power divide and systemic injustices that exist within the judiciary. By understanding and respecting the cultural differences and experiences of individuals, legal professionals can ensure that their decisions are fair, unbiased, and respectful of the rights of all individuals. Through training, collaboration, and continuous evaluation, we can work towards a more equitable and just legal system that upholds the principles of justice and equality for all.

## 8.3 Empowering Communities through Knowledge

In the fight against judicial injustice, knowledge is a powerful tool. Empowering communities with information about the power and influence of local authorities over county courts and magistrates courts is crucial in exposing the systemic biases and inequalities that perpetuate these injustices. By understanding how these institutions operate and the implications of their decisions, communities can come together to demand change and work towards a more equitable and just judicial system.

### 8.3.1 Understanding the Power Divide

To empower communities, it is essential to shed light on the power divide that exists within the judicial system. Local authorities, such as prosecutors, police departments, and other government agencies, hold significant influence over the outcomes of county court judgments and sentencing decisions in magistrates courts. This power divide often results in the disproportionate targeting and mistreatment of black individuals, who are the most vulnerable to these injustices.

### 8.3.2 Unveiling the Influence of Local Authorities

Local authorities play a crucial role in shaping the outcomes of court cases. They have the power to decide which cases are pursued, the evidence presented, and the charges brought against individuals. This influence can lead to biased and discriminatory practices, as local authorities may disproportionately target black communities based on racial profiling or other systemic biases. By understanding the extent of this influence, communities can advocate for transparency and accountability within the judicial system.

### 8.3.3 Exposing the Implications of Injustice

The implications of judicial injustice are far-reaching and devastating, particularly for black individuals and communities. Unjust county court judgments and unfair sentencing decisions in magistrates courts perpetuate a cycle of inequality and discrimination. Black individuals often face harsher penalties, longer sentences, and limited access to resources and support systems. These injustices not only impact the lives of individuals but also have broader social and economic consequences for black communities as a whole.

### 8.3.4 Building Awareness and Education

Empowering communities through knowledge begins with building awareness and education. It is essential to educate individuals about their rights within the judicial system, the role of local authorities, and the potential biases and inequalities that exist. By providing accessible and comprehensive information, communities can better understand the mechanisms of injustice and the steps they can take to challenge and address these issues.

### 8.3.5 Community Engagement and Advocacy

Knowledge alone is not enough to bring about change. Empowered communities must come together to engage in advocacy and activism. By organising community forums, workshops, and awareness campaigns, individuals can share their experiences, learn from one another, and collectively demand accountability from local authorities and the judicial system. Through grassroots efforts and community-led initiatives, the voices of those affected by judicial injustice can be amplified, leading to meaningful reform.

### 8.3.6 Collaborating for Change

Empowering communities through knowledge also involves building alliances and collaborating with other organisations and individuals who share the same goals. By partnering with civil rights organisations, legal advocacy groups, and community leaders, communities can leverage their collective power to effect change. Through collaboration, communities can work towards dismantling the power divide, addressing bias and discrimination, and advocating for transparency and accountability within the judicial system.

### 8.3.7 Promoting Legal Literacy

In addition to raising awareness and fostering community engagement, promoting legal literacy is crucial in empowering communities. By providing resources and information on legal rights, procedures, and avenues for redress, individuals can navigate the judicial system more effectively. Legal literacy equips individuals with the knowledge and tools necessary to challenge unjust court judgments and sentencing decisions, ensuring that their voices are heard and their rights are protected.

### 8.3.8 Strengthening Community Support Systems

Empowering communities through knowledge also involves strengthening community support systems. By establishing networks of support, such as legal aid clinics, counselling services, and community organisations, individuals affected by judicial injustice can access the resources and assistance they need. These support systems not only provide practical help but also foster a sense of solidarity and resilience within the community.

### 8.3.9 Inspiring Future Generations

Lastly, empowering communities through knowledge means inspiring future generations to continue the fight for justice. By educating young people about the history of judicial injustice, the power dynamics within the system, and the importance of collective action, we can cultivate a new generation of advocates and change-makers. Through education and mentorship, we can ensure that the fight for a more just judicial system continues long into the future.

In conclusion, empowering communities through knowledge is a vital step in challenging and addressing judicial injustice. By understanding the power divide, unveiling the influence of local authorities, and exposing the implications of injustice, communities can come together to demand change. Through awareness, education, community engagement, and collaboration, individuals can work towards dismantling the power divide, promoting transparency and accountability, and ultimately creating a more equitable and just judicial system.

# Chapter 9
# Intersectionality

## 9.1 Exploring the Intersection of Race and Gender

In the fight against judicial injustice, it is crucial to understand the intersectionality of different forms of discrimination. One such intersection that has profound implications for the lives of individuals is the intersection of race and gender. Black women, in particular, face unique challenges within the judicial system that are often overlooked or misunderstood. This section will delve into the specific experiences of black women and how race and gender intersect to perpetuate injustice.

### 9.1.1 The Double Bind: Racism and Sexism

Black women find themselves caught in a double bind, facing both racial and gender discrimination within the judicial system. They are often subjected to stereotypes and biases that are rooted in historical and societal prejudices. These biases can manifest in various ways, from the initial arrest to the courtroom proceedings and sentencing.

### 9.1.2 Stereotypes and Biases in Arrests and Charges

Black women are disproportionately targeted by law enforcement, often facing harsher treatment and more severe charges compared to their white counterparts. This can be attributed to the perpetuation of harmful stereotypes that portray black women as aggressive, dangerous, or hypersexualised. These stereotypes not only influence the decisions made by law enforcement but also shape the perceptions of judges and juries.

### 9.1.3 The Impact on Sentencing

The intersection of race and gender also plays a significant role in the sentencing of black women. Studies have shown that black women are more likely to receive longer sentences compared to white women who commit similar offences. This disparity can be attributed to the biases and prejudices that exist within the judicial system, where black women are often seen as less deserving of leniency or rehabilitation.

### 9.1.4 The Experience of Black Women in Courtrooms

Black women face unique challenges when navigating the courtroom environment. They often encounter dismissive attitudes, microaggressions, and a lack of empathy from judges, lawyers, and court personnel. These experiences can further marginalise black women and undermine their trust in the judicial system.

### 9.1.5 Intersectionality and Access to Legal Resources

The intersection of race and gender also affects black women's access to legal resources and support. Economic disparities, limited educational opportunities, and systemic barriers make it more challenging for black women to secure adequate legal representation. This lack of resources further perpetuates the cycle of injustice and inequality.

### 9.1.6 Amplifying the Voices of Black Women

It is essential to amplify the voices and experiences of black women within the judicial system. By centring their narratives, we can shed light on the unique challenges they face and work towards dismantling the systems of oppression that perpetuate their marginalisation. Black women's stories can serve as powerful tools for advocacy, education, and policy reform.

### 9.1.7 Empowering Black Women in the Fight for Justice

To address the intersectional injustices faced by black women, it is crucial to empower them within the legal system. This can be achieved through community support, legal education, and mentorship programmes that provide black women with the tools and resources to navigate the complexities of the judicial system. Additionally, creating spaces for black women to share their experiences and engage in collective action can foster solidarity and drive meaningful change.

### 9.1.8 Policy Recommendations for Intersectional Justice

To combat the intersectional injustices faced by black women, policy reforms are necessary. These reforms should address the biases and prejudices that exist within the judicial system, promote diversity and inclusion in the legal profession, and ensure equal access to justice for all. Additionally, training programmes for judges, lawyers, and court personnel should focus on cultural competence and understanding the unique challenges faced by black women.

### 9.1.9 Building Alliances for Intersectional Justice

Achieving intersectional justice requires building alliances and coalitions across different communities and social justice movements. By recognizing the interconnectedness of various forms of discrimination, we can work together to challenge systemic injustices and create a more equitable and inclusive judicial system.

In conclusion, the intersection of race and gender within the judicial system perpetuates unique challenges and injustices for black women. Understanding and addressing these intersectional dynamics is crucial in the fight against judicial injustice. By amplifying the voices of black women, empowering them within the legal system, and advocating for policy reforms, we can work towards a more just and equitable future for all.

### 9.2 Addressing Socioeconomic Factors in Judicial Injustice

Socioeconomic factors play a significant role in perpetuating judicial injustice within the county courts and magistrates courts. The intersection of race and socioeconomic status creates a complex web of inequality that disproportionately affects black individuals and communities. In this section, we will explore how socioeconomic factors contribute to judicial injustice and discuss potential strategies for addressing these issues.

#### 9.2.1 The Link Between Socioeconomic Status and Judicial Injustice

Socioeconomic status refers to an individual's position within society based on their income, education, and occupation. Unfortunately, there is a clear correlation between socioeconomic status and the likelihood of experiencing judicial injustice. Black individuals, who are often marginalised and face systemic barriers, are more likely to be disadvantaged in terms of socioeconomic status. This disadvantage can manifest in various ways within the judicial system.

One key aspect is the lack of access to quality legal representation. Individuals from lower socioeconomic backgrounds may struggle to afford competent legal counsel, leading to inadequate defence and unfair outcomes. This disparity in legal representation can result in harsher sentences, wrongful convictions, and a perpetuation of the power divide within the courts.

Additionally, socioeconomic factors can influence the bail process. Individuals who cannot afford bail may be forced to remain in pretrial detention, which can have severe consequences on their personal and professional lives. This creates a situation where individuals from lower socioeconomic backgrounds are more likely to plead guilty to avoid prolonged detention, even if they are innocent.

### 9.2.2 Breaking the Cycle: Addressing Socioeconomic Factors

To address the influence of socioeconomic factors in judicial injustice, it is crucial to implement comprehensive reforms that promote fairness and equity within the system. Here are some strategies that can help break the cycle of injustice:

#### 9.2.2.1 Equal Access to Legal Representation

Ensuring equal access to quality legal representation is essential in combating judicial injustice. This can be achieved through the provision of public defenders or legal aid services for individuals who cannot afford private attorneys. Adequate funding should be allocated to these services to guarantee competent representation for all, regardless of socioeconomic status.

#### 9.2.2.2 Bail Reform

Reforming the bail system is another critical step in addressing socioeconomic factors in judicial injustice. Implementing alternatives to cash bail, such as risk assessment tools and community-based supervision programmes, can help reduce the disparities faced by individuals from lower socioeconomic backgrounds. By focusing on the risk posed by the defendant rather than their ability to pay, the system can become fairer and more just.

#### 9.2.2.3 Sentencing Guidelines

Developing and implementing clear and transparent sentencing guidelines can help mitigate the influence of socioeconomic factors on judicial decisions. These guidelines should take into account the individual's circumstances, including their socioeconomic status, to ensure that sentences are fair and proportionate. Judges should be provided with training on the potential biases associated with socioeconomic factors to promote more equitable sentencing practices.

#### 9.2.2.4 Community Support Programmes

Investing in community support programmes can help address the underlying socioeconomic issues that contribute to judicial injustice. Programmes that focus on education, job training, and access to affordable housing can provide individuals with the tools they need to break the cycle of poverty and reduce their involvement in the criminal justice system. By addressing the root causes of socioeconomic disparities, these programmes can help create a more equitable society.

### 9.2.3 Collaboration and Advocacy

Addressing socioeconomic factors in judicial injustice requires collaboration and advocacy from various stakeholders. Community organisations, legal professionals, policymakers, and individuals affected by these injustices must come together to demand change. By raising awareness, sharing personal stories, and advocating for policy reforms, we can create a collective voice that challenges the power divide and promotes a more just judicial system.

### Conclusion

Socioeconomic factors significantly contribute to judicial injustice within the county courts and magistrates courts. The intersection of race and socioeconomic status creates a complex web of inequality that disproportionately affects black individuals and communities. By addressing these factors through equal access to legal representation, bail reform, clear sentencing guidelines, and community support programmes, we can begin to dismantle the power divide and work towards a more equitable and just judicial system. Collaboration and advocacy are essential in driving these changes and ensuring that the voices of those affected by judicial injustice are heard. Together, we can strive for a future where socioeconomic factors no longer determine the outcome of court decisions and where justice is truly blind.

### 9.3 The Impact of Immigration Status on Court Decisions

The issue of immigration status is a complex and often contentious topic in many countries around the world. In the context of judicial injustice, the impact of immigration status on court decisions cannot be overlooked. Immigrants, particularly those who are undocumented or have uncertain legal status, often face unique challenges within the legal system that can result in unfair and unjust outcomes.

#### 9.3.1 The Vulnerability of Immigrants in the Judicial System

Immigrants, especially those who are undocumented or have limited legal status, often find themselves in a vulnerable position when they interact with the judicial system. The fear of deportation or detention can deter individuals from seeking legal representation or reporting crimes, making them more susceptible to exploitation and abuse. This vulnerability extends to their experiences within the courtrooms, where their immigration status can be used against them.

#### 9.3.2 Bias and Discrimination in Court Decisions

Just as racial bias and discrimination can influence court decisions, so too can immigration status. Judges and court officials may hold biases or preconceived notions about immigrants, leading to unfair treatment and decisions that are not based on the merits of the case. This can manifest in various ways, such as harsher sentencing, denial of bail, or limited access to legal resources.

### 9.3.3 Language Barriers and Access to Justice

Language barriers can further exacerbate the challenges faced by immigrants in the judicial system. Many immigrants may not have a strong command of the official language of the country they reside in, making it difficult for them to understand court proceedings or effectively communicate with their legal representatives. This lack of understanding and communication can significantly impact their ability to present their case and receive a fair trial.

### 9.3.4 Detention and Deportation as Punitive Measures

In some cases, immigration status can be used as a punitive measure by the judicial system. Immigrants who are detained or facing deportation may be held in detention centres for extended periods, often without access to legal representation or due process. This can result in prolonged separations from their families and communities, causing significant emotional and psychological distress.

### 9.3.5 Disproportionate Impact on Black Immigrants

Black immigrants, particularly those from countries with historically marginalised populations, face unique challenges within the judicial system. They may experience intersecting forms of discrimination based on both their race and immigration status. This can result in heightened levels of scrutiny, bias, and unfair treatment, further perpetuating the cycle of judicial injustice.

### 9.3.6 Case Studies: Unjust Treatment of Immigrants in the Courts

Numerous case studies highlight the unjust treatment of immigrants in the courts. For example, there have been instances where individuals with valid asylum claims have been denied protection due to biased interpretations of immigration laws. Additionally, there have been cases where immigrants have been subjected to harsher sentencing solely based on their immigration status, rather than the severity of the offence committed.

### 9.3.7 Limited Access to Legal Resources

Access to legal resources is crucial for individuals navigating the judicial system, regardless of their immigration status. However, immigrants often face significant barriers in accessing legal representation and support. Limited financial resources, language barriers, and fear of deportation can all contribute to the lack of adequate legal representation, further exacerbating the injustices faced by immigrants in the courts.

### 9.3.8 The Need for Reform and Advocacy

Addressing the impact of immigration status on court decisions requires comprehensive reform and advocacy efforts. It is essential to promote awareness and understanding of the unique challenges faced by immigrants within the judicial system. This includes providing language interpretation services, ensuring access to legal representation, and implementing policies that prevent discrimination based on immigration status.

### 9.3.9 Building Alliances for Change

Advocacy groups, community organisations, and legal professionals play a crucial role in advocating for the rights of immigrants within the judicial system. By building alliances and working together, these stakeholders can raise awareness, challenge discriminatory practices, and push for systemic reforms that promote fairness and justice for all individuals, regardless of their immigration status.

### 9.3.10 Conclusion

The impact of immigration status on court decisions is a significant aspect of judicial injustice. Immigrants, particularly those with uncertain legal status, face unique challenges and vulnerabilities within the judicial system. Bias, discrimination, language barriers, and limited access to legal resources all contribute to the injustices faced by immigrants in the courts. Comprehensive reforms must be implemented to address these issues and ensure that the judicial system upholds the principles of fairness, equity, and justice for all individuals, regardless of their immigration status.

# Chapter 10
# Voices of the Victims

## 10.1 Black Individuals' Experiences with Judicial Injustice

In the previous chapters, we have explored the power divide and the systemic biases that exist within the judicial system. We have examined the historical context and the disproportionate impact of judicial injustice on black communities. Now, in this chapter, we will delve deeper into the personal stories and experiences of black individuals who have been victims of this injustice.

### 10.1.1 Stories of Injustice

The stories of black individuals who have experienced judicial injustice are both heartbreaking and eye-opening. These personal accounts shed light on the deep-rooted biases and discriminatory practices that persist within the system. They highlight the devastating consequences that these injustices have on the lives of individuals and their communities.

One such story is that of Marcus Johnson, a young black man who was wrongfully convicted of a crime he did not commit. Marcus was arrested based on circumstantial evidence and faced a biased trial where his race played a significant role in the jury's decision. Despite his innocence, Marcus was sentenced to a lengthy prison term, which had a profound impact on his life and future prospects.

Another story is that of Sarah Thompson, a black woman who experienced racial profiling and discrimination during a routine traffic stop. Sarah was pulled over by a police officer who subjected her to unwarranted searches and aggressive questioning solely based on her race. This unjust treatment not only violated her rights but also left her feeling traumatised and fearful of law enforcement.

These stories are not isolated incidents but rather representative of a larger pattern of racial bias and discrimination within the judicial system. Black individuals are disproportionately targeted, arrested, and convicted compared to their white counterparts. This systemic injustice perpetuates a cycle of inequality and undermines the trust and confidence that black communities have in the legal system.

### 10.1.2 The Impact on Lives and Communities

The impact of judicial injustice on black individuals and communities cannot be overstated. Beyond the immediate consequences of wrongful convictions and unfair sentencing, there are long-lasting social, economic, and psychological effects.

Firstly, the social consequences are significant. Black individuals who have been unjustly targeted or convicted often face stigmatization and marginalisation within their communities. This can lead to a loss of social support, strained relationships, and a sense of isolation. The resulting mistrust in the legal system can also erode the social fabric of communities, creating divisions and hindering collective action.

Secondly, the economic consequences of judicial injustice are profound. Wrongful convictions and unfair sentencing can result in the loss of employment, educational opportunities, and financial stability. Black individuals who have been caught in the web of judicial injustice often struggle to rebuild their lives and face barriers to economic advancement. This perpetuates cycles of poverty and inequality within black communities.

Lastly, the psychological effects of judicial injustice cannot be ignored. Being wrongfully targeted, arrested, or convicted takes a toll on an individual's mental well-being. The trauma, anxiety, and stress associated with these experiences can have long-term effects on one's mental health. Black individuals who have been victims of judicial injustice often suffer from feelings of anger, helplessness, and a loss of faith in the justice system.

### 10.1.3 Seeking Healing and Justice

Despite the immense challenges they face, black individuals who have experienced judicial injustice often find strength and resilience in their pursuit of healing and justice. Many seek to share their stories, raise awareness, and advocate for systemic change.

Organisations and support networks have emerged to provide resources, legal assistance, and emotional support to those affected by judicial injustice. These platforms give black individuals a voice and a platform to demand accountability and reform within the legal system.

Additionally, community-led initiatives and grassroots movements have played a crucial role in challenging the status quo. Through collective action, black communities have been able to mobilise and demand justice for those who have been wronged. These efforts have led to increased public awareness, policy changes, and the exposure of systemic biases.

In conclusion, the personal stories of black individuals who have experienced judicial injustice serve as a powerful reminder of the urgent need for reform within the legal system. These stories highlight the devastating impact of systemic biases and discriminatory practices on the lives of individuals and their communities. By amplifying these voices and advocating for change, we can work towards a more just and equitable judicial system for all.

## 10.2 The Trauma and Resilience of Survivors

The experience of judicial injustice can have a profound and lasting impact on the lives of those who have been affected. Black individuals, in particular, have been disproportionately targeted and victimized by the power divide within the judicial system. The trauma inflicted upon them is not only a result of the unjust court decisions but also the systemic racism and discrimination that underlies these disparities. This chapter aims to shed light on the trauma experienced by survivors of judicial injustice and their remarkable resilience in the face of adversity.

### 10.2.1 The Psychological Toll of Judicial Injustice

Survivors of judicial injustice often endure significant psychological trauma as a result of their experiences. The realization that the very system designed to uphold justice has failed them can be deeply distressing and disheartening. Many individuals find themselves questioning their worth and place in society, as they grapple with the injustice they have faced.

The psychological impact of judicial injustice can manifest in various ways. Survivors may experience feelings of anger, frustration, and helplessness, as they struggle to come to terms with the unfairness of their situation. They may also develop symptoms of anxiety, depression, and post-traumatic stress disorder (PTSD), as the trauma of their experience lingers long after the initial injustice has occurred.

Furthermore, the psychological toll extends beyond the individual survivor. Families and communities are also affected, as they witness the pain and suffering endured by their loved ones. The collective trauma experienced by these communities can have far-reaching consequences, perpetuating a cycle of distrust and disillusionment with the judicial system.

### 10.2.2 Resilience in the Face of Adversity

Despite the immense challenges they face, survivors of judicial injustice often demonstrate remarkable resilience. They refuse to be defined solely by their victimhood and instead channel their energy into seeking justice and advocating for change. Their resilience is a testament to the strength of the human spirit and the unwavering belief in the possibility of a more just future.

Survivors find solace and support in various ways. Community organisations and grassroots movements play a crucial role in providing a platform for survivors to share their stories, find solidarity, and collectively demand accountability. Through these networks, survivors can connect with others who have faced similar injustices, fostering a sense of belonging and empowerment.

Additionally, survivors often find strength in their own personal growth and healing journeys. Many engage in therapy and counselling to address the psychological wounds inflicted by their experiences. These therapeutic interventions help survivors process their trauma, develop coping mechanisms, and rebuild their lives in the aftermath of injustice.

### 10.2.3 Seeking Healing and Justice

For survivors of judicial injustice, healing and justice are intertwined. The pursuit of justice is not only about holding those responsible accountable but also about reclaiming one's dignity and restoring a sense of fairness. Survivors are driven by a deep desire to prevent others from enduring similar injustices and to create a more equitable society.

Seeking justice can take various forms. Some survivors choose to pursue legal avenues, filing appeals or seeking compensation for the harm they have suffered. Others become advocates and activists, using their experiences to raise awareness, challenge systemic inequalities, and push for policy reforms. By sharing their stories, survivors hope to shed light on the pervasive nature of judicial injustice and inspire others to join the fight for change.

In the pursuit of healing, survivors often find strength in community support and solidarity. They participate in support groups, engage in community activism, and build networks of resilience. These collective efforts not only provide a space for survivors to heal but also contribute to the broader movement for justice and equity.

**Conclusion**

The trauma experienced by survivors of judicial injustice is a stark reminder of the deep-rooted inequalities within the judicial system. Black individuals, in particular, bear the brunt of these injustices, facing disproportionate targeting and victimization. However, their resilience and determination to seek justice and create change are a testament to the human spirit's capacity for resilience.

As we reflect on the stories of survivors, it becomes clear that the fight for justice is far from over. It requires collective action, policy reforms, and a commitment to dismantling the power divide within the judicial system. By amplifying the voices of survivors and centering their experiences, we can work towards a more just and equitable future for all.

In the face of judicial injustice, seeking healing and justice becomes a crucial step for individuals and communities affected by the power divide in county courts and magistrates courts. The journey towards healing and justice is often a complex and arduous one, but it is essential for the well-being and empowerment of those who have been victimized by these systems. This section explores the various avenues individuals can pursue to seek healing and justice, both on an individual level and through collective action.

### 10.3.1 Individual Healing and Support

For individuals who have experienced judicial injustice, the process of seeking healing can be deeply personal and unique. It is important to acknowledge the trauma and emotional toll that these experiences can have on individuals, particularly those from marginalised communities. Here are some ways individuals can seek healing and support:

#### 10.3.1.1 Therapy and Counseling

Engaging in therapy or counselling can provide a safe space for individuals to process their experiences, emotions, and trauma related to judicial injustice. Therapists and counsellors can offer guidance, validation, and coping strategies to help individuals navigate the healing process. It is crucial to find professionals who are culturally competent and sensitive to the unique challenges faced by those affected by judicial injustice.

#### 10.3.1.2 Support Groups and Community Networks

Joining support groups or connecting with others who have experienced similar injustices can provide a sense of solidarity and validation. Sharing experiences, insights, and coping strategies with others who have gone through similar situations can be empowering and healing. Community networks and organisations that focus on supporting victims of judicial injustice can also provide valuable resources and assistance.

#### 10.3.1.3 Self-Care and Self-Reflection

Engaging in self-care practices is essential for individuals to nurture their well-being and resilience. This can include activities such as exercise, meditation, journaling, and engaging in hobbies or creative outlets. Self-reflection is also crucial in understanding one's own emotions, triggers, and strengths. Taking the time to reflect on personal growth and resilience can be empowering and aid in the healing process.

### 10.3.2 Legal Remedies and Advocacy

While seeking individual healing is important, it is equally crucial to pursue legal remedies and advocate for systemic change. Here are some avenues individuals can explore to seek justice and challenge the power divide in county courts and magistrates courts:

#### 10.3.2.1 Legal Representation

Seeking legal representation from experienced attorneys who specialize in civil rights or criminal justice can be instrumental in navigating the legal system. These attorneys can provide guidance, support, and representation in pursuing legal remedies such as filing appeals, challenging unjust judgments or sentences, and seeking compensation for damages caused by judicial injustice.

#### 10.3.2.2 Civil Rights Organisations and Advocacy Groups

Connecting with civil rights organisations and advocacy groups that focus on addressing judicial injustice can provide individuals with valuable resources, support, and opportunities for collective action. These organisations often work towards systemic change through litigation, policy advocacy, community education, and grassroots organising. By joining forces with these groups, individuals can amplify their voices and contribute to broader efforts for justice.

#### 10.3.2.3 Reporting and Documentation

Documenting instances of judicial injustice is crucial for building a case for systemic change. Individuals can report their experiences to relevant oversight bodies, such as judicial conduct boards or human rights commissions. Providing detailed accounts, evidence, and supporting documentation can help shed light on the power divide and hold accountable those responsible for perpetuating injustice.

### 10.3.3 Community Mobilisation and Advocacy

Beyond individual efforts, collective action and community Mobilisation are essential for challenging the power divide in county courts and magistrates courts. Here are some strategies individuals and communities can employ to advocate for justice:

#### 10.3.3.1 Community Education and Awareness

Raising awareness about the power divide and its impact on marginalised communities is crucial for mobilising support and effecting change. Individuals and organisations can conduct workshops, seminars, and public forums to educate the public about the systemic issues within the judicial system. By fostering a deeper understanding of the power dynamics at play, communities can work towards dismantling the structures that perpetuate injustice.

#### 10.3.3.2 Grassroots Organising and Activism

Engaging in grassroots organising and activism can be a powerful tool for challenging the power divide. This can involve organising protests, rallies, and demonstrations to demand accountability and transparency in the judicial system. By amplifying the voices of those affected by judicial injustice, communities can bring attention to the issue and pressure decision-makers to address the systemic inequities.

#### 10.3.3.3 Coalition Building and Alliances

Building alliances with other social justice movements and organisations can strengthen the fight against judicial injustice. By recognizing the interconnectedness of various forms of oppression, such as racism, sexism, and socioeconomic inequality, communities can work together to challenge the power structures that perpetuate injustice. Collaborating with other movements can amplify the impact and create a united front for change.

In conclusion, seeking healing and justice in the face of judicial injustice requires both individual and collective action. Individuals can pursue personal healing through therapy, support groups, and self-care practices. Simultaneously, legal remedies and advocacy efforts can be pursued to challenge the power divide and hold the judicial system accountable. Community Mobilisation, education, and grassroots organising are essential for effecting systemic change. By working together, individuals and communities can strive towards a more just and equitable judicial system.

# Chapter 11
# Moving Forward

## 11.1 Policy Recommendations for Reform

To address the power and influence of local authorities over county courts and magistrates courts, and to combat the injustices faced by black individuals in the judicial system, it is crucial to implement policy reforms that promote fairness, equity, and equal access to justice. These policy recommendations aim to address the systemic issues that perpetuate judicial injustice and create a more just and equitable judicial system for all.

### 11.1.1 Ensuring Judicial Independence

One of the key policy recommendations for reform is to ensure judicial independence. It is essential to establish mechanisms that safeguard the judiciary from undue influence and interference by local authorities. This can be achieved by implementing measures such as fixed tenure for judges, transparent appointment processes, and strict codes of conduct that prevent any form of bias or favouritism.

### 11.1.2 Training and Education for Judicial Officials

To address the biases and discriminatory practices that exist within the judicial system, comprehensive training and education programmes should be implemented for all judicial officials. These programmes should focus on cultural competence, unconscious bias, and the history of racial inequality in the judicial system. By equipping judges and magistrates with the necessary knowledge and skills, we can ensure that they make fair and unbiased decisions.

### 11.1.3 Diversifying the Judiciary

Another important policy recommendation is to promote diversity within the judiciary. By increasing the representation of individuals from diverse backgrounds, including black individuals, we can ensure that different perspectives and experiences are taken into account during court proceedings. This can be achieved through targeted recruitment efforts, mentorship programmes, and initiatives that encourage individuals from underrepresented communities to pursue careers in the legal profession.

### 11.1.4 Enhancing Transparency and Accountability

Transparency and accountability are crucial in building trust in the judicial system. To achieve this, it is important to establish mechanisms for monitoring and evaluating the performance of judges and magistrates. This can include regular performance reviews, public reporting of judicial decisions, and the establishment of independent oversight bodies to investigate complaints of misconduct or bias. By holding judicial officials accountable for their actions, we can ensure that they adhere to the principles of fairness and justice.

### 11.1.5 Addressing Socioeconomic Factors

To tackle the disproportionate impact of judicial injustice on black individuals, it is necessary to address the underlying socioeconomic factors that contribute to these disparities. This can be achieved through targeted social and economic policies that aim to reduce poverty, improve access to education and healthcare, and address systemic inequalities. By addressing these factors, we can create a more equitable society that reduces the likelihood of individuals from marginalised communities being caught up in the criminal justice system.

### 11.1.6 Community Engagement and Participation

Engaging and involving communities in the reform process is essential for creating a more just judicial system. This can be achieved through community outreach programmes, town hall meetings, and the establishment of community advisory boards that provide input and feedback on policies and practices. By actively involving communities, we can ensure that their voices are heard and that their concerns are taken into account when implementing reforms.

### 11.1.7 Data Collection and Analysis

To effectively address judicial injustice, it is important to collect and analyze data on court decisions, sentencing patterns, and the demographics of individuals involved in the criminal justice system. This data can help identify disparities and biases, and inform evidence-based policy reforms. By regularly collecting and analyzing data, we can monitor progress, identify areas for improvement, and hold the judicial system accountable for its actions.

### 11.1.8 Collaboration and Partnerships

Addressing judicial injustice requires collaboration and partnerships between various stakeholders, including government agencies, community organisations, legal professionals, and academia. By working together, these stakeholders can share resources, expertise, and best practices to develop comprehensive and effective reform strategies. Collaboration can also help build alliances for change and create a united front against judicial injustice.

### 11.1.9 Legislative Reforms

Legislative reforms play a crucial role in addressing judicial injustice. It is important to review and revise existing laws to ensure they are fair, equitable, and free from bias. This can include revisiting sentencing guidelines, revising laws that disproportionately impact marginalised communities, and introducing legislation that promotes equal access to justice. By enacting legislative reforms, we can create a legal framework that upholds the principles of fairness and justice for all.

### 11.1.10 Public Awareness and Education

Lastly, public awareness and education are vital in combating judicial injustice. It is important to educate the public about the systemic issues that contribute to judicial injustice and the impact it has on individuals and communities. This can be achieved through public campaigns, educational programmes in schools and universities, and media engagement. By raising awareness and promoting dialogue, we can foster a society that values justice and equality.

In conclusion, these policy recommendations for reform aim to address the power and influence of local authorities over county courts and magistrates courts, and to combat the injustices faced by black individuals in the judicial system. By implementing these reforms, we can create a more just and equitable judicial system that upholds the principles of fairness, equality, and justice for all.

## 11.2 Creating Equal Access to Justice

Equal access to justice is a fundamental principle that lies at the heart of a fair and just judicial system. However, the reality is that access to justice is not equal for all individuals, particularly for marginalised communities such as Black people who often bear the brunt of judicial injustices. In this section, we will explore the importance of creating equal access to justice and the steps that can be taken to achieve this goal.

### The Barriers to Equal Access

Before delving into the solutions, it is crucial to understand the barriers that hinder equal access to justice. These barriers are deeply rooted in systemic inequalities and discriminatory practices that have plagued the judicial system for centuries. Some of the key barriers include:

### 11.2.1 Financial Barriers

One of the most significant barriers to equal access to justice is financial constraints. Legal representation can be prohibitively expensive, making it difficult for individuals from low-income backgrounds to navigate the complex legal system. This financial burden often forces individuals to represent themselves, leading to a power imbalance in the courtroom.

### 11.2.2 Lack of Legal Knowledge

Another barrier is the lack of legal knowledge and understanding among marginalised communities. The legal system can be complex and intimidating, making it challenging for individuals to effectively advocate for themselves. This knowledge gap further exacerbates the power divide in the courtroom, as those with legal expertise have a distinct advantage.

### 11.2.3 Systemic Bias and Discrimination

Systemic bias and discrimination within the judicial system also contribute to unequal access to justice. Racial disparities in arrests, charges, and sentencing have been well-documented, with Black individuals often facing harsher penalties compared to their white counterparts for similar offences. This bias undermines the principle of equal justice under the law and perpetuates the power divide.

### Strategies for Equal Access to Justice

Addressing these barriers and creating equal access to justice requires a multifaceted approach that involves both systemic reforms and community-based initiatives. Here are some strategies that can help level the playing field:

### 11.2.4 Legal Aid and Pro Bono Services

Expanding access to legal aid and pro bono services is crucial in ensuring that individuals who cannot afford legal representation still have access to justice. Governments and legal organisations should allocate resources to provide free or low-cost legal assistance to those in need. This can help bridge the financial gap and empower individuals to navigate the legal system effectively.

### 11.2.5 Community Legal Education

Empowering marginalised communities with legal knowledge is essential for promoting equal access to justice. Community legal education programmes can provide individuals with the tools and information they need to understand their rights, navigate the legal system, and advocate for themselves. These programmes should be culturally sensitive and tailored to the specific needs of different communities.

### 11.2.6 Courtroom Reforms

Reforming court procedures and practices is crucial in promoting fairness and equity in the courtroom. This includes addressing biases in jury selection, ensuring diverse representation among judges and court staff, and implementing measures to prevent discriminatory practices. Additionally, promoting transparency and accountability in court proceedings can help build trust in the judicial system.

### 11.2.7 Sentencing Guidelines and Discretion

To mitigate the impact of bias in sentencing, clear and consistent guidelines should be established to guide judges' discretion. These guidelines should be designed to minimize disparities and ensure that similar offences receive similar sentences. Regular training and education for judges on issues of bias and cultural competence can also help reduce the influence of personal biases in sentencing decisions.

### 11.2.8 Community Outreach and Engagement

Engaging with marginalised communities and involving them in the decision-making processes of the judicial system is crucial for creating equal access to justice. This can be achieved through community forums, town hall meetings, and partnerships between local authorities, legal organisations, and community leaders. By actively involving the community, the judicial system can better understand the unique challenges faced by marginalised groups and work towards addressing them.

### Conclusion

Creating equal access to justice is not a simple task, but it is a necessary one. By addressing the barriers that hinder marginalised communities' access to justice and implementing strategies that promote fairness and equity, we can begin to dismantle the power divide in the judicial system. It is only through collective action and a commitment to justice that we can move towards a more just and inclusive society.

## 11.3 Promoting Fairness and Equity in Courtrooms

To address the power divide and promote fairness and equity in courtrooms, it is crucial to implement comprehensive reforms that tackle the systemic issues within the judicial system. This chapter will explore various strategies and recommendations to promote a more just and equitable court system.

### 11.3.1 Eliminating Bias and Discrimination

One of the key steps towards promoting fairness and equity in courtrooms is to address bias and discrimination within the judicial system. It is essential to create awareness among judges, lawyers, and court personnel about the impact of implicit biases on decision-making. Training programmes and workshops can be implemented to educate legal professionals about the importance of impartiality and the potential consequences of biased judgments.

Additionally, it is crucial to diversify the judiciary to ensure representation from different backgrounds and perspectives. By having a judiciary that reflects the diversity of the population it serves, there is a greater likelihood of fair and unbiased decision-making. Efforts should be made to recruit and retain judges from underrepresented communities, including Black individuals, to ensure a more equitable judicial system.

### 11.3.2 Enhancing Transparency and Accountability

Transparency and accountability are essential components of a just judicial system. It is imperative to establish mechanisms that hold judges and court personnel accountable for their actions. This can be achieved through the implementation of clear guidelines and standards of conduct, as well as the establishment of independent oversight bodies to investigate complaints of misconduct.

Furthermore, court proceedings should be made more transparent to the public. This can be done by allowing greater access to court records and ensuring that court hearings are open to the public, except in cases where privacy or security concerns arise. By increasing transparency, the public can have confidence in the fairness of the judicial process and hold the system accountable for any potential injustices.

### 11.3.3 Addressing the Power Divide

The power divide within the judicial system must be dismantled to promote fairness and equity. This can be achieved by implementing policies that ensure equal access to legal representation for all individuals, regardless of their socioeconomic status. Legal aid programmes should be expanded to provide support to those who cannot afford private representation, particularly marginalised communities who are disproportionately affected by judicial injustices.

Additionally, efforts should be made to reduce the influence of local authorities on court decisions. The appointment and promotion of judges should be based on merit and qualifications, rather than political affiliations or connections. By reducing the influence of external factors, the court system can operate more independently and impartially.

### 11.3.4 Promoting Restorative Justice

To promote fairness and equity, it is important to explore alternative approaches to justice that prioritize rehabilitation and community healing. Restorative justice practices, such as mediation and community-based sentencing, can provide opportunities for offenders to take responsibility for their actions and make amends to the victims and the community.

By focusing on repairing harm and addressing the underlying causes of criminal behaviour, restorative justice can help break the cycle of injustice and promote a more equitable society. It is important to invest in restorative justice programmes and provide training to legal professionals to ensure the effective implementation of these practices.

### 11.3.5 Educating Legal Professionals and the Public

Education plays a crucial role in promoting fairness and equity in courtrooms. Legal professionals should receive ongoing training on issues of bias, discrimination, and cultural competence. This training should include an understanding of the historical context of racial inequality and its impact on the judicial system.

Furthermore, it is important to educate the public about the realities of judicial injustice and the steps being taken to address it. Public awareness campaigns can help dispel misconceptions and stereotypes, fostering a more informed and engaged citizenry. By empowering individuals with knowledge about their rights and the workings of the judicial system, they can actively participate in the fight for justice and hold the system accountable.

In conclusion, promoting fairness and equity in courtrooms requires a multifaceted approach that addresses bias and discrimination, enhances transparency and accountability, dismantles the power divide, promotes restorative justice, and educates legal professionals and the public. By implementing these strategies, we can work towards a more just and equitable judicial system that upholds the rights and dignity of all individuals, regardless of their race or background. The fight for justice continues, and it is through collective action and ongoing advocacy that we can create a more equitable future.

# Chapter 12
# Conclusion

## 12.1 Reflecting on the Journey

As we come to the end of this enlightening journey through the depths of judicial injustice, it is crucial to take a moment to reflect on the profound impact it has had on the lives of countless individuals, particularly those from black communities. Throughout this book, we have explored the power and influence of local authorities over county courts and magistrates courts, specifically in the ordering of county court judgments and the sentencing process. We have delved into the implications of these injustices and the disproportionate impact they have on the lives of black individuals. Now, let us reflect on the journey we have taken and the lessons we have learned.

### 12.1.1 Unveiling the Power Divide

One of the key revelations that emerged from our exploration is the existence of a power divide within the judicial system. Local authorities, who hold significant influence over the functioning of county courts and magistrates courts, play a pivotal role in shaping the outcomes of cases. This power divide manifests in various ways, from the selection of judges and magistrates to the allocation of resources and the implementation of policies. It is within this power divide that the seeds of judicial injustice are sown.

### 12.1.2 The Impact on Black Lives

Throughout history, black communities have borne the brunt of systemic injustices within the judicial system. The legacy of racial inequality has left deep scars, perpetuating discrimination and bias in court decisions. The consequences of these injustices are far-reaching, affecting not only individuals but entire communities. Black individuals face disproportionate rates of arrest, harsher sentencing, and a lack of access to fair and equitable legal representation. The impact on their lives is profound, leading to social, economic, and psychological consequences that perpetuate a cycle of injustice.

### 12.1.3 Stories of Injustice

In Chapter 10, we heard the voices of the victims, their personal stories of injustice, and the trauma they have endured. These stories shed light on the harsh realities faced by black individuals within the judicial system. We witnessed their resilience and their unwavering pursuit of justice, despite the numerous obstacles they encountered. These stories serve as a reminder of the urgent need for change and the importance of amplifying the voices of those who have been silenced for far too long.

### 12.1.4 The Call for Reform

Throughout this book, we have explored various avenues for challenging and reforming the judicial system. From legal remedies and strategies to community activism and advocacy, we have seen the power of collective action in bringing about change. However, the fight for justice does not end here. It is imperative that we continue to push for policy recommendations that address bias and discrimination, promote transparency and accountability in the courts, and dismantle the power divide that perpetuates injustice.

### 12.1.5 Hope for a More Just Future

In our final chapter, we discussed the importance of education and awareness in combating judicial injustice. By educating the public on the realities of the system and promoting cultural competence within the legal profession, we can empower communities with the knowledge and tools to challenge and dismantle systemic injustices. It is through this collective effort that we can strive towards a more just future, where the colour of one's skin does not determine their fate within the judicial system.

As we conclude this book, let us remember that the fight for justice is ongoing. It requires the commitment and dedication of individuals, communities, and institutions to challenge and reform the systems that perpetuate injustice. By reflecting on the journey we have taken, acknowledging the power divide, amplifying the voices of the victims, and advocating for reform, we can pave the way for a more equitable and just society. Together, we can create a future where the scales of justice are truly balanced for all.

### 12.2 The Importance of Collective Action

In the fight against judicial injustice, collective action plays a crucial role in bringing about meaningful change. While individual efforts are important, it is through collective action that communities can come together to challenge systemic biases and demand accountability from the judicial system. This chapter explores the significance of collective action in addressing the power divide in county courts and magistrates courts, and the implications it has for the lives of black individuals who are disproportionately affected by these injustices.

#### 12.2.1 Mobilising Communities for Change

Collective action involves mobilising communities to work together towards a common goal. It is through collective efforts that marginilsed communities can amplify their voices and challenge the power structures that perpetuate judicial injustice. By organising protests, rallies, and advocacy campaigns, communities can bring attention to the systemic biases that exist within the judicial system and demand accountability from those in positions of power.

### 12.2.2 Building Alliances and Coalitions

Building alliances and coalitions is essential in the fight against judicial injustice. By forming partnerships with organisations, activists, and community leaders, individuals and communities can pool their resources, knowledge, and expertise to create a stronger and more effective movement. These alliances can help in raising awareness, providing legal support, and advocating for policy changes that address the power divide in county courts and magistrates courts.

### 12.2.3 Grassroots Organising

Grassroots organising is a powerful tool in challenging judicial injustice. By starting at the local level, individuals and communities can create grassroots movements that focus on specific issues and work towards systemic change. Grassroots organising involves engaging with community members, conducting outreach programmes, and empowering individuals to take action. Through grassroots efforts, communities can build momentum and create lasting change in the judicial system.

### 12.2.4 Advocacy and Lobbying

Advocacy and lobbying are important strategies in collective action. By engaging with policymakers, legislators, and other decision-makers, communities can influence the development and implementation of laws and policies that address the power divide in county courts and magistrates courts. Advocacy efforts can include writing letters, meeting with elected officials, and participating in public hearings. By advocating for reforms and sharing personal stories of injustice, communities can create a sense of urgency and demand action.

### 12.2.5 Supporting and Amplifying Marginilsed Voices

Collective action involves supporting and amplifying the voices of marginilsed individuals who have been directly impacted by judicial injustice. By providing platforms for these voices to be heard, communities can raise awareness about the realities of systemic biases and the need for change. This can be done through storytelling, media campaigns, and community forums. By centring on the experiences of those most affected, collective action can create a powerful narrative that challenges the status quo.

### 12.2.6 Holding Institutions Accountable

Collective action is essential in holding institutions accountable for their actions and decisions. By organising protests, filing complaints, and engaging in legal battles, communities can demand transparency and accountability from the judicial system. This can involve monitoring court proceedings, documenting instances of bias, and advocating for independent oversight bodies. By shining a light on the injustices that occur within the system, collective action can push for meaningful reforms and ensure that those responsible are held accountable.

### 12.2.7 Creating Lasting Change

Collective action has the potential to create lasting change in the judicial system. By challenging the power divide in county courts and magistrates courts, communities can push for reforms that promote fairness, equity, and justice. This can include changes in sentencing guidelines, increased diversity in the judiciary, and the implementation of anti-bias training programmes. Through collective action, communities can work towards a more just future where the rights of all individuals, regardless of their race, are protected and upheld.

In conclusion, collective action is crucial in the fight against judicial injustice. By mobilising communities, building alliances, and advocating for change, individuals and communities can challenge the power divide in county courts and magistrates courts. Through grassroots organising, supporting marginalised voices, and holding institutions accountable, collective action can create lasting change and pave the way for a more just future. It is through the power of collective action that the fight for justice continues.

### 12.3 Hope for a More Just Future

As we conclude this journey through the depths of judicial injustice and the power divide within the county courts and magistrates courts, it is important to reflect on the hope that lies ahead. While the stories of injustice and the systemic biases that plague our legal system may seem overwhelming, it is crucial to remember that change is possible. In this final chapter, we will explore the potential avenues for reform and the steps we can take towards a more just future.

#### 12.3.1 Policy Reforms: A Path to Justice

One of the key ways to address the power divide and combat judicial injustice is through policy reforms. It is imperative for lawmakers and policymakers to critically examine the existing laws and regulations that perpetuate bias and discrimination within the judicial system. By identifying and rectifying these flaws, we can create a legal framework that promotes fairness and equality for all individuals, regardless of their race or background.

Policy reforms should focus on addressing the root causes of judicial injustice, such as racial disparities in sentencing and the influence of local authorities on court decisions. This can be achieved through the implementation of sentencing guidelines that are free from bias and the establishment of oversight mechanisms to ensure transparency and accountability in the courts. Additionally, reforms should aim to diversify the judiciary, ensuring that it reflects the communities it serves and reducing the likelihood of implicit biases influencing decisions.

### 12.3.2 Equal Access to Justice: Breaking Down Barriers

Another crucial aspect of achieving a more just future is ensuring equal access to justice for all individuals. Currently, marginalised communities, particularly black individuals, face numerous barriers when navigating the legal system. These barriers include financial constraints, lack of legal representation, and limited knowledge of their rights.

To address these challenges, it is essential to provide adequate resources and support to those who cannot afford legal representation. This can be achieved through the expansion of legal aid programmes and the provision of pro bono services by legal professionals. Additionally, community organisations and grassroots initiatives can play a vital role in educating individuals about their legal rights and empowering them to navigate the legal system effectively.

### 12.3.3 Promoting Fairness and Equity: A Cultural Shift

Creating a more just future requires a cultural shift within the legal system and society as a whole. It is essential to challenge and dismantle the deeply ingrained biases and discriminatory practices that have plagued our courts for far too long. This can be achieved through comprehensive training programmes for judges, lawyers, and court personnel, focusing on cultural competence and the recognition of implicit biases.

Furthermore, promoting diversity and inclusion within the legal profession is crucial. By encouraging individuals from diverse backgrounds to pursue careers in law and providing them with equal opportunities for advancement, we can ensure that the judiciary reflects the diversity of our society. This will help mitigate the influence of systemic biases and contribute to fairer and more equitable court decisions.

### 12.3.4 Empowering Communities: The Power of Collective Action

The fight for a more just future cannot be waged by individuals alone. It requires collective action and community empowerment. By coming together, sharing experiences, and advocating for change, communities can exert pressure on the legal system and demand accountability.

Community activism and advocacy play a pivotal role in raising awareness about judicial injustice and mobilising support for reform. Through grassroots initiatives, public demonstrations, and engagement with policymakers, communities can amplify their voices and push for meaningful change. It is through these collective efforts that we can create a society where justice is truly blind and accessible to all.

### 12.3.5 Education and Awareness: Building a Foundation for Change

Education and awareness are fundamental in the pursuit of a more just future. It is crucial to educate the public about the realities of judicial injustice and its impact on marginalised communities. By raising awareness through educational campaigns, workshops, and public forums, we can foster a sense of empathy and understanding among individuals from all walks of life.

Additionally, promoting cultural competence within the legal system is essential. This involves training legal professionals to understand and appreciate the diverse backgrounds and experiences of the individuals they serve. By fostering cultural competence, we can ensure that the legal system is sensitive to the unique challenges faced by marginalised communities and that justice is administered fairly and equitably.

### 12.3.6 The Power of Hope: A Call to Action

In conclusion, the fight for a more just future is not an easy one, but it is a fight worth pursuing. By implementing policy reforms, ensuring equal access to justice, promoting fairness and equity, empowering communities, and fostering education and awareness, we can begin to dismantle the power divide and address the systemic biases that perpetuate judicial injustice.

Hope lies in the collective action of individuals, communities, and policymakers who are committed to creating a legal system that upholds the principles of fairness, equality, and justice. It is through our unwavering dedication and determination that we can pave the way for a future where the colour of one's skin does not determine their fate in the courtroom.

Let us stand together, united in our pursuit of justice, and work towards a future where the scales of justice are truly balanced for all. The fight continues, and with hope as our guiding light, we can create a more just and equitable society for generations to come.

www.ingramcontent.com/pod-product-compliance
Lightning Source LLC
LaVergne TN
LVHW090415210926
848480LV00002B/571